An Illustrated Diary of Its Most Exciting Years

MEN, MONEY, AND MACHINES

BOOK TWO

A division of American Family Enterprises, Inc.

Robert Schramke—Publisher
Alan C. Hahn—Marketing Director
Robert Whiteman—Editorial Consultant
Marilyn Appleberg—Managing Editor
Ada Bardossi—Contributing Editor
Miriam Berman—Book Design
Susan McQuibben—Picture Research

The Stonehouse Press—Production Supervision

Library of Congress Catalog Card Number 72-94255

PICTURE CREDITS

Brown Bros. 13, 46; Courtesy Sunkist 100; Courtesy of RCA 25; General Motors 77; Library of Congress 31, 46, 48, 52, 53, 54, 66, 73; Merck & Co. 59, 62; Movie Star News 37, 92, 93; Photo World 24, 26, 27, 56; Smithsonian 18; UPI 12, 14, 15, 16, 17, 18, 19, 20, 25, 27, 28, 29, 30, 31, 34, 35, 36, 42, 44, 45, 46, 49, 50, 55, 58, 61, 63, 74, 75, 87, 94, 95, 97, 98, 104, 105, 106, 110, 112, 113, 118, 124, 125, 126, 127, 128, 129, 130, 131, 132, 133, 134, 135, 136, 138, 139, 140; U.S. Army 67, 69, 78, 79, 80, 81, 82, 83, 84, 85, 106, 114, 115, 116, 117, 122, 123, 128; U.S. Information 72, 107, 121; U.S. Mint 111; Westinghouse 64; Wide World 40, 41, 86; Art: Cliff Condak 17, 23, 38-39, 70, 88-89, 101, 102, 109.

Printed in the United States of America

23456789987654321

Table of Contents

MEN, MONEY, AND MACHINES

INTRODUCTION

The two decades between the mid-thirties and the mid-fifties were dramatic ones. There was the good, and there was the bad. The good? Advances in science, medicine, transportation. The bad? Two wars.

Even before the mushroom cloud appeared over Hiroshima in 1945, science had made tremendous strides in many fields. Some discoveries turned out to be both harmful and beneficial. Microfilm, for example, was a tool of espionage agents. It was also to be a means of preserving books and newspapers in our libraries.

Radar was a means of locating enemy targets in wartime. Later it became a standard safety measure on commercial airlines. Penicillin, which saved lives late in the war years, is routinely used in medicine today. The splitting of the atom was envisioned by the physicists who accomplished it as a help to civilization instead of the horror it was in 1945. Afterward many peacetime uses were found for this discovery.

The rockets sent aloft from Peenemünde to devastate London have evolved into the rockets used to send space vehicles aloft to explore the universe. The television that is a cause of many battles between parents and offspring came out of this period, too. And, thanks to TV, doctors can monitor patients, teachers can command wide student audiences, current events can be seen over the world while they are happening, and man can see other men walking on the moon.

The rapid improvement in automobiles was halted during the Second World War, when the assembly lines were converted to making bombers and fighter planes. When automaking was resumed after V-J Day, cars became faster, so better highways were needed. There are those who think America is well on its way to being a vast superhighway and parking lot. But, stung by safety conscious gadflies, Detroit is putting in features that may help us get where we are going in safety as well as in record time.

Hollywood was still in its great era in the thirties and forties, and DeMille and Goldwyn were great names as well as colorful legends. We find here stories about both of them.

It was an interesting, challenging time to be alive—not always happy, but far from dull. This volume of AMERICA presents a sampling of the financial, technical, and entertainment side of life in the early Atomic Age. Read it, and let it bring back memories . . .

Are American Women Holding Aviation Back?

by Amelia Earhart

Amelia Earhart, the first woman to fly across the Atlantic, discusses safety in the sky and her sex's timorous way of keeping their menfolk from using the air lanes.

The world's first airline stewardesses.

In the last few years I have addressed many defenseless audiences throughout America. My lecturing chiefly concerns flying experiences of my own, for people seem most to desire personal anecdotes. Usually, however, I impose at least one brief "sermon" about commercial aviation—everyday air travel—and almost always I ask three questions to be answered by raised hands.

"How many in this audience have been in an airplane within the last three years?" I have been asking that question for a long time now, and it is remarkable how the proportion of affirmative response has increased.

"If I were able to give you a free ride on an established air line to some place you'd like to go and return, how many would accept?" That usually brings ninety per cent or more of upraised hands.

The third question is the one that interests me most: "How many would not?"

Usually fewer than ten per cent of the audience would not fly, even as guests. These are for the most part older people. And usually, alas, they include more women than men. In fact, the most resistant persons to air travel I have found are those who have everything to make them liberal— *i.e.*, older women's social clubs.

Of course my informal research is restricted to "cases" who turn out to hear a flyer talk—cases who, it is fair to suppose, are above the average in their interest in aviation. Still, the proportion holds true generally, for air lines find that women actually do offer the greatest "sales resistance" to commercial flying in America. Having been an executive of two passenger-carrying air lines, I have rubbed shoulders pretty intimately with that problem.

Basic Problem

At present twenty to thirty per cent of the aviation traveling public are women. That means that in the current year two hundred thousand women in America will use air transportation. Normally more men than women travel on trains, busses, and steamships. But I believe the male preponderance aloft is larger in proportion.

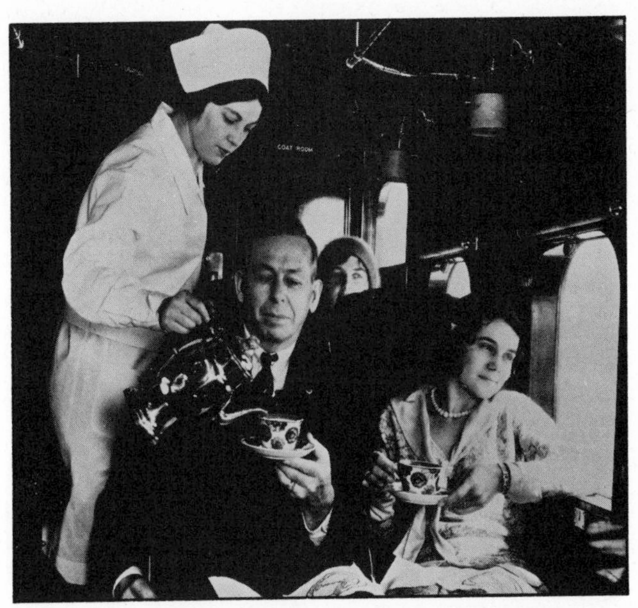

Early stewardesses wore nurses' uniforms.

Persuading more women to fly as passengers is not, however, the basic problem of the air lines, pleasant as would be an increase in feminine ticket buying. The trouble is that women too often not only will not travel by air themselves but try to keep their menfolk from doing so.

Such an attitude is not unnatural. Because of inheritance and training and the barriers maintained around women for so long, it is inevitable that we, as a sex, should be invested with some special timidities. Lack of knowledge or unfamiliarity often breeds fear. However, the emancipation of modern women is rapidly changing such characteristics. A girl's upbringing today differs from that of her grandmother as much in independence of attitude as in scholastic subject matter. Her viewpoint and her willingness—nay, her eagerness—to try new things rival that of her brothers.

To the modern child, girl or boy, there is no great wonder in aviation. It is as routine to them as the automobile is to their parents, whose parents in turn saw the automobile replace horse-drawn vehicles, many no doubt rebelling at the innovation and the inherent "dangers" of gasoline propulsion.

I often point out an oxcart is far safer than

Amelia Earhart in a rare publicity pose (top). (Bottom) Andrew Mellon congratulates Miss Earhart on being the first woman to fly the Atlantic.

an automobile. Yet oxcarts do not flourish on the ribboned highways. It is statistically true that for speeds in excess of forty-five miles an hour one is safer on the air lines than on the highway. Last year air lines in America flew a total of 313,905,508 passenger miles and carried 746,946 passengers. There were only fifty-eight accidents and fifteen passenger fatalities, which means that one has to fly 20,927,034 miles before one's turn comes for a fatality. In other words, if one flew 1,0000 miles a day every day in the year, it would be fifty-eight years before one might expect fatal injury.

Exact statistics covering the proportion of men and women air travelers weren't kept until recently, but from the information available it seems fair to estimate that the proportion of women travelers on the air lines in the last five years has increased from about five per cent to twenty or thirty per cent. Certainly in the last two years, according to two major transcontinental lines, there has been an increase of at least five per cent.

Time-Saving-Element

Mrs. Franklin D. Roosevelt is without doubt one of the most consistent women air travelers. She finds the time-saving element all-important in her busy life. I had the pleasure of flying with Mrs. Roosevelt three years ago—I think on her first night flight. We came directly from dinner, wearing light evening clothes, and the fact that we hopped into the big plane "as was" caused some amused comment. To both of us the circumstance simply emphasized the casualness of air travel.

Today there is no more need of special clothing for air passengers (or indeed air pilots) on the air lines than there is for one who travels in a comfortable limousine or Pullman. However, because so many miles are covered in so short a time, it is well to think of clothes in terms of the end as well as the beginning of a journey. Literally a few hours may take one from winter to summer.

Naturally the women who use the air lines most are women in business. A notable piler-up of air miles is Mrs. Estelle Gilbert of a Los Angeles department store. I know that a few months ago she had completed forty-five trips

Upon return from London Amelia Earhart was greeted by a cheering crowd at the Boston airport.

First class luxury isn't anything new in air transportation. Old 21 passenger DC-3 (l) could be converted into a 14-passenger skylounger with deep cushioned swivel chairs.

across the United States with TWA. Incidentally, she reckoned that in the time saved she had effected an economy for her employer of more than eight thousand dollars.

Business women do not do all the flying. Women traveling for pleasure are among regular air-line customers; and the number of children carried with or without mothers is remarkable. One factor in this development is the presence of the transcontinental lines of stewardesses, all of whom are registered nurses.

Service The Baby

To illustrate the modern attitude, Mr. Putnam reports a conversation which took place on his last trip to California. As the plane taxied to a stop at a Midwest city, the stewardess said to the mother of an infant in arms:

"Now you get off here and relax a few moments. I'll service the baby."

My husband could not resist chiming in.

"Servicing the baby sounds as if you meant to grind valves and change oil," he said.

"Well, the company overhauls the motors periodically," the stewardess replied; "why not the passengers?"

As a matter of fact, babies seem to thrive aloft. And there are many traveled youngsters who have had far more hours in the air than

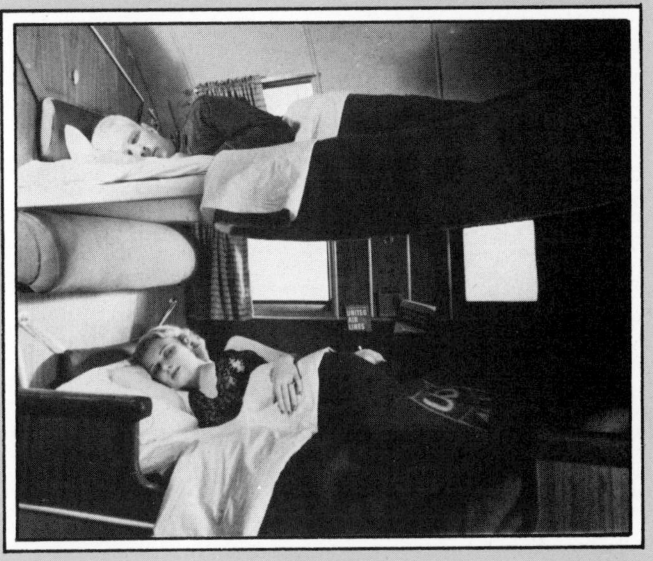

Another 1930-era innovation was coast-to-coast sleeper service. During the day cabins were divided into compartments (l). At night seats converted into upper and lower berths.

on trains. Certainly if I were sending young children or old people, to whom any kind of travel is uprooting, I should use the air lines to curtail the journey's length and ease the strain.

Aside from passengers, a number of women are directly connected with the business of flying, in the air as well as on the ground. United Air Lines, who pioneered in placing stewardesses on their planes, now have two hundred and fifty attractive young women in their personnel. When United first inaugurated its long-distance night service, the company employed seven stewardesses. From an average of three per cent women travelers, the passenger lists soon showed ten per cent—a figure which since then has doubled.

New Profession

Moreover, this new profession has opened another employment niche for women to fill, and a particularly alluring one.

Increasingly the air lines are striving to make the women of America conscious of the attractiveness of modern commercial flying. One of the most original gestures to that end is TWA's gift of a gardenia corsage to every woman as she leaves the plane. Is it any wonder the percentage of women passengers is increasing?

Henry Ford Tells His New Faith in America

by William L. Stidger

When Henry Ford was interviewed in 1935, the country was still in the midst of depression. But he nevertheless set his production goal high.

We have faith in America out here in Dearborn. We have so much faith that we have set as our production goal one million new cars—or more. This is the highest goal we have set in four years. As far as we are concerned the depression is over and we are going forward in that faith and on that assumption this year. The last year that we passed the million mark was 1930, when we made 1,485,000 cars.

I feel that when the depression is over in our thinking, it will be over for the whole country. If American industrialists had faith in the American people and in the great resources of American individualism, and if American business men would stop looking for a Santa Claus and would take firm hold of their own business organizations and run them with good sound common American horse sense, you would see results in a hurry.

During the next ten months we are putting $5,500,000 into capital improvements which have already commenced and which will about double the power capacity of our River Rouge plant. This indicates more than anything I can say that our attitude is one of confidence.

That expenditure was made necessary by the enlargement of the steel plant at the River Rouge. When all of the collateral requirements of this forward move are fulfilled we will have expended $10,000,000 with other concerns throughout the country in machinery and services of various sorts. No industry can receive benefits without dispensing benefits. The only question is, *who is to start the movement?* Some are entirely willing to distribute benefits after they have received benefits. But that way is not always successful. You must give before you can receive. The getters are always losing: it is the givers who stay in the game. The best giving is investing.

The least any one can do is to try and give as much as you get. Now, that applies to the hiring of men. If you hire a man for the purpose of pumping out of him everything you can get, the chances are you will get mighty little. It is better to begin by putting something into the man you hire. The farmer knew, without having to go to an agricultural school, that you had to feed the soil to get a crop. He also learned that at certain times you had to let fields lie fallow for a year or two. The depression might be looked upon as our fallow years. Considered in that way they would have been useful to us. As a matter of fact that is precisely the use we made of the depression in our company. We began to do things we had been too busy to do before. We opened a new chapter in automobile history as a result of it. The V-8 car came out of that period. You can bemoan a depression, or you can use it.

Always keep a child or a man doing something a little in advance of what he thinks he can do. There are some men who always think themselves little until the right man comes along and asks them to do something big—and they do it. A boy told me the other day—his name was Jackie—that he learned to swim by falling into the Rouge River and finding he had to swim or go down. We have learned in this nation during the last four years that we "can take it," as the boys say, and that it takes a lot of doing to hurt these United States. That is one reason we of Dearborn have not shown any fear of what has happened—and that also is the reason why I have faith in the immediate future of America. The far-off future everybody agrees is safe. But the

immediate future is safe too. Wise men are getting ready to start *now*.

Every man who came to this country in its early days was an individualist. Every pioneer who settled it and opened up the West was an individualist. It is always the desire of individuals to have a chance at freedom and to carve out their own lives. We are all the descendants of that kind of people, and we are still pioneering. There are other wildernesses to conquer besides those our forefathers found.

Cannot Regiment Us

When people try to take individualism out of the average American they are trying the impossible. It simply cannot be done. The American people will not be regimented because they can't be. Other nations may be quite agreeable to such a process, but not the people of America. The so-called foreigners who have come to us in the last century were all individualists. In fact, most of them came here to escape regimentation.

It is most interesting to note who it is that asks us to eliminate individualism from the American people. We usually find that the very persons, or leaders, who propose to regiment us are themselves the most unregimented among us. The three typical regimenters of the world today—they are all outside America—are perhaps the most outstanding individualists on earth.

What our own would-be American regimenters propose to do about their own extreme

(Below) Original home of Ford Motor Company. (r) Henry Ford, founder of the corporation.

In 1938 The Ford Motor Company expanded its operations to the tune of $34,000,000. Part of that expansion program included a plant for the construction of new tires.

individualism they do not tell any one. Are they so convinced of its evil that they are willing to sacrifice it along with ours? They are prescribing for us but not for themselves. They have as their goal reducing our people to masses, but they evidently have it in their minds to remain the masters. Of course this event will not come off.

As we look back and see our own people coming into this wilderness more than 300 years ago, their every attitude and act is marked by initiative. Every man jack of them was a self-starter. They had to carve out their own destinies. They had no machines, no bosses, no one to look to but themselves. If they wanted houses, they had to build them. If they wanted food, they had to grow it. Nothing was done *for* them. They had to do everything for themselves. They grew and prospered. This nation was founded by individual initiative.

Create What We Need

Government overseas feared their progress and tried to prevent it. The colonists were forbidden to import machinery. So they created their own. The first patent granted on our soil was given on a device invented by a farmer's wife. If you have ever studied our collections of Americana at Dearborn, you have seen how every kitchen in the colonies gave evidence of the inventive genius of the American. Nothing could stop the spirit of self-help.

Now, the only hope of the American people is to revive those qualities. We still have them. The strain of stock and breed in a tree, a horse, a man, and in a nation is indestructible. I have always believed that the American people are the pioneer essence of all the nations represented here, and that essence does not evaporate. The qualities that brought them here are still within them. There is no substitute for them. Our national mistake has been that we ever thought there could be any substitute for them. When the cardinal and inclusive quality of individualism begins to stir again, as surely it will, in our 125,000,000 individual Americans, we shall see the nation move forward.

That is what I expect to see this coming year. That is why I believe in the immediate future of this nation. This country is going to need all the production it can get. Overproduction? Everything has been underproduced and overpriced.

We are going to see lavish production of high-quality goods in every line at prices every one can pay so that every one may be supplied. That is a condition this country has never seen as yet, but it is coming.

Henry Ford and his son Edsel (r) introduce their new 1934 Model V-Eight Ford.

You'll Soon See Across the Sea

by David Sarnoff

David Sarnoff knew his television, and in 1937 issued this progress report.

It was good to hear your voice, but we would have been better pleased to see you with us," I called to Senator Marconi through my desk microphone in Radio City across five thousand miles of ether. "We will soon be able to *see* each other by transatlantic television," retorted the Father of Radio from his yacht *Electra* in the Mediterranean. This prediction was his most salient contribution to an extraordinary four-cornered conversation. The other participants, flying between Washington, D.C., and Buffalo, New York, in separate planes, were Robert Jardillier, the French Minister of Communications, and Maurice Rambert, president of the International Broadcasting Union.

The radio short wave was the djin that carried our voices almost instantaneously across oceans and continents. It linked three modern marvels—airplane, radio broadcasting, and transatlantic radiotelephone.

Radio, it is true, has grown a century in ten years. Will television grow as fast as Marconi's brain child has grown? Shall we really be able *soon* to *see* each other across the ocean? That is a matter of speculation. "Soon" may be five or ten years; maybe more. Television is today where radio broadcasting was in the first year of its existence. It has been for years a reality in the laboratory. It is on the point of becoming a practical reality in the sphere of education and entertainment. But, in spite of astonishing forward strides made even in the last six months, it is not yet here for the public at large. I said in the summer of 1936 that the size of the image transmitted by our present equipment was not large enough to be enjoyed by more than a small gathering. I pointed out that the broadcasting range was fifteen to twenty-five miles. Developments since that time have been somewhat more rapid than I anticipated. The size of the image reflected on the television screen has been increased and the effective station range has been lengthened in one instance to forty-five miles.

Experimental television broadcasts are now being carried on from our NBC studios in the RCA Building. We broadcast actual scenes, staged in our television studio, as well as "canned pictures," reproductions, usually somewhat curtailed, of movie films. We *telecast* not only vaudeville acts but newsreels and speeches.

TV Prefers Blondes

The television artist must have not merely a voice but a presentable personality; he must be an actor as well as a speaker or singer. Television, like radio, requires a special technique. In the first television experiments chalk-white faces, black eyebrows, and black lips were required. This ghastly make-up has been discarded in favor of a panchromatic scheme, employing chiefly various shades of pale orange, red, and brown. These colors reproduce well on the screen; they give an even tone to the skin and accentuate the artist's features. Light waves prefer blondes! At least, for the time being, blondes are reproduced most flatteringly on the "kinescope" screen.

It is even possible that this characteristic, unless we can correct it, will have an effect on the fortunes of political candidates in the future. The radio played an important part in the recent Presidential campaign; it is not too bold a speculation to say that the next Presidential campaign, four years hence, may be influenced by television.

The present television screen is too small to permit the adequate transmission of mass

David Sarnoff and Guglielmo Marconi in 1933

Early television set

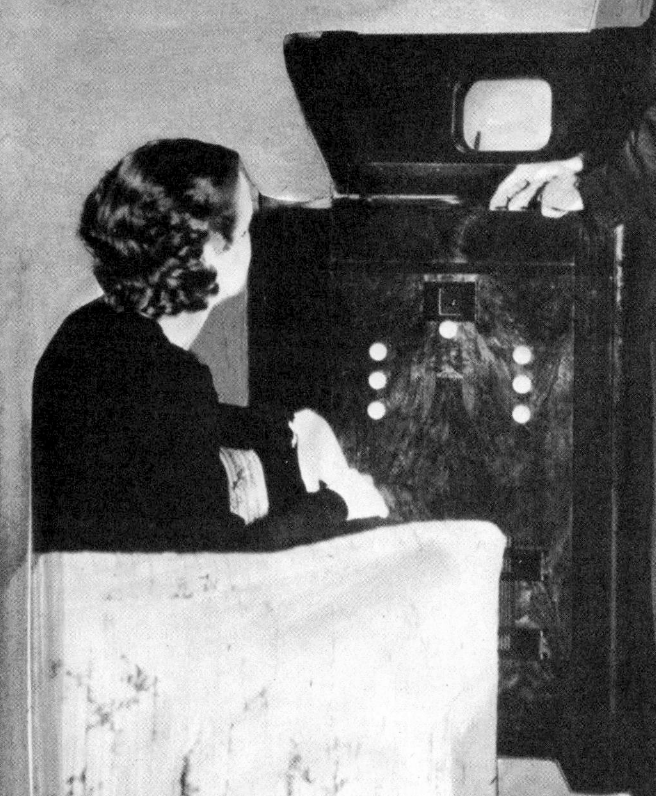

scenes, parades, processions. If more than two or three actors appear on the scene simultaneously they are reduced in size, and detail is lost, although playlets with five actors, occupying the stage simultaneously, have been successfully televised. If we magnify the television picture beyond a certain point, the sharpness of definition decreases.

How Television Works

The smallness of the television image does not deprive the scene of reality, because everything is in proportion. The general effect is that of watching a moving picture. Television pictures are yellow, or greenishly tinted. The typical television set looks like an ordinary full-sized radio with a mirror on the inside of the cover reflecting the image screen. The most recent machines have a twelve-inch kinescope and are capable of reproducing pictures of seven and a half by ten inches. Fifteen or twenty people can easily gather around an ordinary television receiver in its present stage and enjoy the synchronized sound and light effects.

In various demonstrations we have used fifteen receivers to entertain two or three hundred people. Sound and sight waves were sent from our studio in Radio City to the Empire State tower and sent back from there to our black-draped laboratory NBC theater in Radio City. Television films are placed in projection machines and run off exactly like moving pictures.

French track star Roger Rochard is interviewed on an early television program.

The magic transformation from picture to electric signal is wrought through the "iconoscope tube" and the "iconoscope camera." The iconoscope camera changes the speaker or actor from a visual thing into so many electric impulses. High-frequency tubes amplify the picture signals. We use "audio" transmitters for sound and "video" transmitters for sight. (*Audio* is Latin for "I hear"; *video* for "I see.") Sound and sight are transmitted simultaneously. "Antenna filters" make it possible to transmit sight and sound from a single antenna. Dials similar to those on the radio set tune in sound and picture signals.

We use two methods for transmitting our programs: In one, the "radio link," the image rides through the air. The other system transmits the image by what is known as the "coaxial cable." The first is based on the principle of wireless; the second on that of the telephone. It is too early to say which of the two methods will finally be adopted. For the present we utilize both experimentally.

We have tested television chiefly in the metropolitan area and adjacent suburbs. These tests have disclosed various requirements that must be met by commercial service. We have learned a great deal about ultra-short waves and interferences. Our engineers have surmounted the difficulties involved in the task of making the apparatus function outside the laboratory. Our experiments have confirmed the soundness of the technical fundamentals upon which we propose to build television.

Standards of television transmission and reception have been steadily improved. The recent RCA field tests have employed "343-line definition"; that is, each separate picture (of which there are thirty a second) is made by an electronic beam racing across the screen in a series of 343 horizontal lines. RCA and the other members of the Radio Manufacturers' Association have now recommended to the Fed-

Felix The Cat was the subject most used during experimental telecasts in the 1920s.

eral Communications Commission the adoption of even finer definition, that of 441 lines, as the commercial standard. It is of course essential that all television transmitters operate according to a single standard, in order that a receiving set may be tuned to any broadcasting station within range.

Various European countries are experimenting successfully with television. From the point of view of research, laboratory development, and technical progress, the United States leads its European rivals. In European countries television is subsizided by various governments; the areas involved are comparatively small. In the United States television is backed by free individual initiative and private capital.

TV Uses Limitless

If television were to progress no further it could serve certain limited purposes even today. It could entertain patients in hospitals, invalids, and others debarred for any reason from leaving their domiciles. It provides even now thrills for the amateur.

Television will play an important part in education. It will transmit, even more vividly than the radio, the messages of culture and science. Lecturers will be heard and seen simultaneously in 10,000 lecture halls. Statesmen of the next decade should be able to see and talk to each other as if they were gathered around the same table, without leaving their capitals.

The time may come when medical experts will not be compelled to travel hundreds of miles in emergencies; they will be able to see the patient and discuss his case with the doctor without leaving their clinics. Doctors are frequently consulted by telephone or, on the high seas, by radio. But the car cannot entirely take the place of the eye.

Executives who now communicate by teletype and radio with their staffs will be able to transmit their orders to ear and eye; they will be able to know what is going on in any part of their plant by pressing a button. These are a few possibilities. Actually it is impossible to foretell the extent to which television will modify civilization. Primarily television programs will serve the purpose of public entertainment and education.

Eventually television will bring not only the people of the United States but the people of the world closer together. The more contact we establish with nations and individuals, the more we multiply the avenues through which the brain is approached, the easier it should be to reconcile conflicting national and economic interests.

(Right) tennis stars Les Stoefen and Frank Shields appear on television show back in 1934; (below) although it never took the country by storm, phone-a-vision was invented in late 1930s.

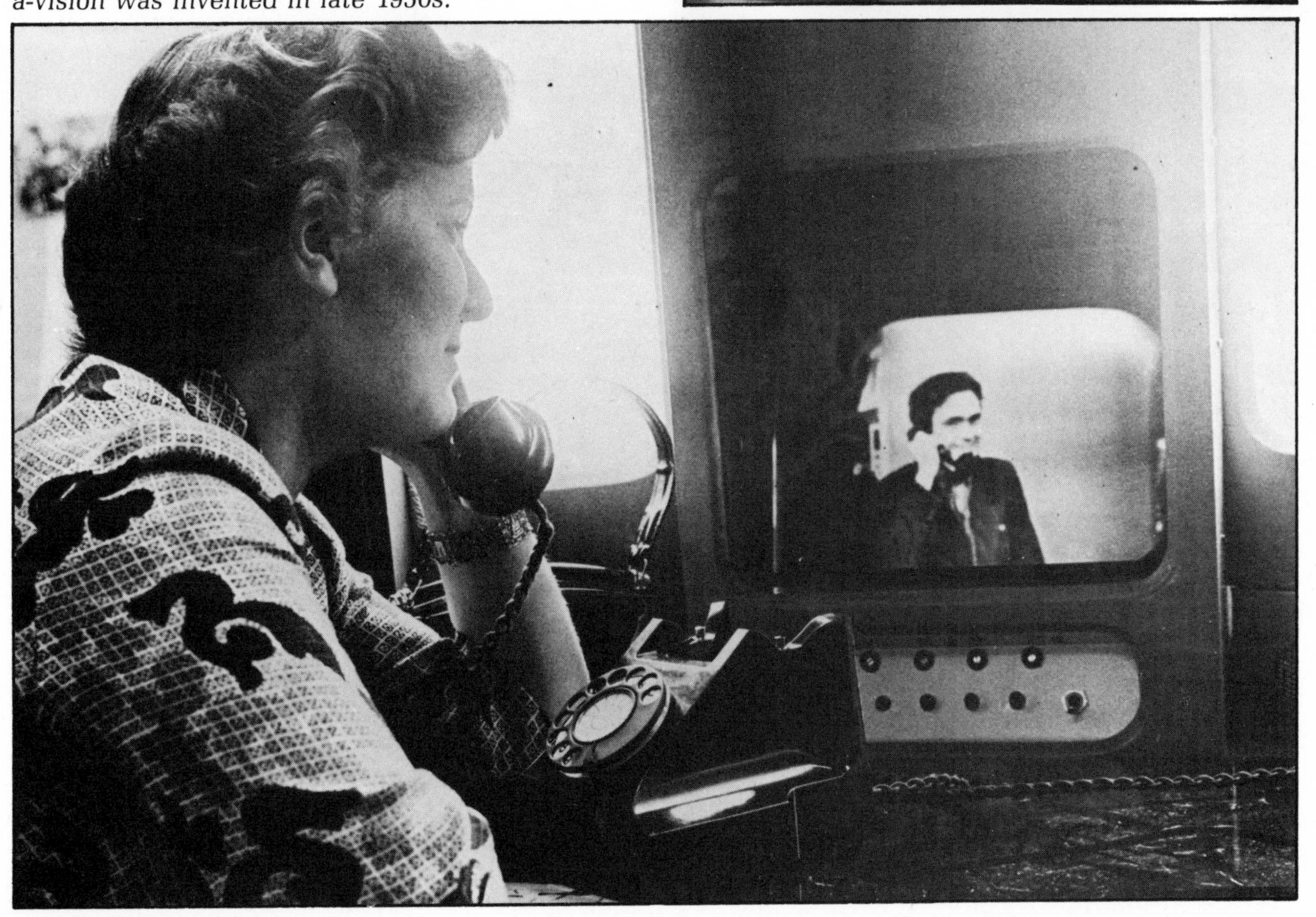

The Crown Jewels of America

by W. J. Cameron

It was early in 1941 and America had not yet entered the war. But people were taking a long look at our heritage, and W. J. Cameron put some of their thoughts into words.

Rumors were heard during the past year that the crown jewels of one or another country were being removed to other lands for safety. Now, no royal crown or scepter or orb, no throne or sword of state exists in this country—nonetheless we have crown jewels of more than regal splendor and of priceless worth. What are they?

Some might answer that those precious writings, the Declaration of Independence and the Constitution of the United States are our high insignia of state. But in these matters our nation was somewhat like ourselves—in *youth* we seldom are interested in our genealogy or our family heirlooms; *that* appreciation comes with maturity. So the Declaration of Independence and other precious documents lay neglected by this young nation for 100 years, exposed to fire and weather hazards, until the Centennial of 1876, when Americans began to reflect on the formative period of their history. Many other things were more highly treasured than these documents at first—things that preceeded them and things that flowered from them.

There's the shrine of Plymouth Rock where the weary Pilgrims landed; there's a country

Souther and Mercy Barnes, descendants of the original Pilgrims, view Plymouth Rock where their forefathers landed from the Mayflower.

A monument to Mother Nature: the Yosemite Falls in California's Yosemite National Park.

church at Richmond where epic words were spoken that burn with meaning yet; there's the Old North steeple, Boston, where the signal lanterns hung; there's a river bridge at Concord where once the embattled farmers stood; there are pleasant dells at Valley Forge where the winter snow lay heavy; there's a room in Philadelphia where grave men wisely wrought; there's a farm on the Potomac where our Cincinnatus lived; there's a cherished spot at Yorktown where a storied struggle ended; there's a Hermitage in Tennessee whence a lionheart emerged; there's the Alamo in Texas, mute memorial of sacrificial gallantry; there's a cabin in Kentucky where an emancipator first beheld the light. These are some of the crown jewels of America.

Yet these are not all. Among the Rockies there are cloud-capped peaks named for men that made them signposts for the westward-faring people. There are handcarts at Salt Lake City, dragged a thousand miles over prairie and mountain by men and women seeking freedom. There are missions and harbors and cities all up and down the Pacific coast sacred to the pioneers. And then the landmarks of American enterprise—from the early iron forges and milling machinery of Pennsylvania and the cotton gin of Georgia, to the electrical wizardry of Edison that lighted the world from New Jersey, and the giant irrigation dams that, as works of man, excel the pyramids. At the San Francisco Fair a gold spike was exhibited, of greater worth than gold, because it symbolized the pony track widening to the wagon track and that hardening into the railroad track of the nation's westward progress. These also are among the crown jewels of America.

And yet there are more. Little schools that grew into famous universities; pioneer medical practices that made a noble science and profession; the whole American system of free and universal education; the expanding American economy, giving greater value for a lower price and higher wages for less burdensome labor than any other in the world; freedom to speak and to print, freedom to assemble and think and worship, freedom to say "no" as well as "yes" and vote as conscience dictates; a nation devoted to the social art of living together in peace, a nation owning its homes, a nation unafraid—these also are among our crown jewels of America.

We may think of these and we may think of this rich land of our heritage that can abundantly provide for all. We may think of our flag—look at that flag! Women and children never have fled in terror before that flag! We may think of our temple of covenanted liberties—the Constitution—for a century and a half an impregnable dike against encroachments of power.

Who can name or number the crown jewels of our nation? If you would see them all, then you must see every city and village, every street, every shop and farm and home. The crown jewels of America are everywhere.

Mt. Rushmore, in the Black Hills of South Dakota, is man's largest memorial to man.

Early Settlers' Monument and Minuteman Statue (top left and right). Stonington, Connecticut Square and Fisherman's Memorial Monument at Glouster (bottom left and right).

Hollywood Miracle Man

by Frederick Van Ryn

It was the same Cecil B. DeMille, but this colorful personality always made good reading. This article appeared in 1942.

A stockily built man, of medium height, dashed up a long flight of stairs leading to a wooden platform, covered the distance separating him from the public address system in two seconds flat, came to a stop in front of the mike, surveyed his audience of some five hundred stars, starlets, extras, electricians, and stagehands, and then, after what seemed like centuries of suspense, opened his mouth and let the epithets fly.

His immaculate white sports shirt, beautifully tailored breeches, and very high boots suggested a polo player rather than a motion-picture director, but his gift of invective left no doubt as to his identity. Only two men in modern history could have delivered that unrehearsed and unprepared oration—Huey P. Long and Cecil B. De Mille. But Mr. Long was dead. So it could only have been the formidable C. B.

He minced no words in describing his anguish, nay, his despair, at the sight of so much pigheadedness gathered on a single motion-picture lot. He recalled the existence of his five-year-old grandson, and admitted cheerfully that he would shoot him without a moment's hesitation if he became convinced that the dear lad was as hopeless a half-wit as the grown-ups he was addressing now. He pointed out that at the rate they were progressing (or should he say "retrogressing"?) that morning, it was certain that come 1945, they would still be wasting his good money and their wretched time.

The warm-up period over, he was about to fire the first real salvo when his eagle eye fell on a young little thing standing in the rear of the crowd. It seemed to him—he hoped he was wrong—that he had caught her in the heinous act of whispering in the ear of a girl by her side. He stopped short. He made a few steps backward. He studied the gorgeously polished boots that would have gladdened the heart of the hardest taskmaster in the United States cavalry. He shook his head as if trying to convince himself that the whole tragic episode was only a bad dream. He groaned, and then he spoke up again.

"Young lady," he said. "Yes, I mean you, way back there in the green dress. Come here at once."

The poor little thing blinked, trembled, looked helplessly at her neighbors, then started making her way slowly through the crowd. With the burning eyes of the Great Inquisitor still riveted on her bloodless face, she arrived at her grim destination.

What She Really Said

"Young lady," he thundered in a voice that the millions who tune in each Monday night on the Lux Radio Theater program would never have recognized as that of their velvety master of ceremonies, "I hate to inconvenience you, but the trouble is, I am so stupid and inefficient that I can't talk and listen at the same time. So go to the mike and repeat for the benefit of all of us the supremely important message that you simply had to transmit to your girl friend."

The girl sighed. She was ready to break into tears when something, probably Mr. De Mille's warlike boots, made her realize that hers, after all, was a race of fighters.

"Do you really want me to repeat what I said?" she queried, half tremblingly, half challengingly.

"I certainly do."

"Every single word?"

"Every single word."

Cecil B. DeMille listens as Charlton Heston thunders off stage lines in Ten Commandments.

(Top) Cecil B. works with his secretary Gladys Rosson. (Bottom) his Hollywood home.

"Very well," said the girl. "I said 'I wish to heaven the old louse would stop gabbing and let us have lunch.' "

For a split second Mr. De Mille remained motionless. Then (he must have realized that even the magician whose sixty-six supercolossal epics had grossed fifty-five million dollars for Paramount could not possibly hope to top that heartfelt remark) he raised his right hand stiffly and said, "Company dismissed for lunch."

P.S. The girl was not fired.

And now that we have had our first glimpse of the only man in the history of the motion-picture industry who succeeded in defying time and tide and the law of gravity, let us follow him around the clock.

It's 7 A.M. The rambling old-fashioned house where the creator of *The Ten Commandments* has lived and dreamed and raved for the past twenty-four years is awake. It's really two houses connected by a long glass-enclosed passageway. One of them is used as De Mille's personal quarters, the other as offices.

C. B. is up. The sounds coming from his part of the building indicate that a free-for-all fight is taking place in the great man's bedroom, but the servants are not worried. They know that all that racket and commotion and bang-bang simply means that the master is exercising. So fantastic are the paraphernalia De Mille uses for his morning calisthenics that no one, not even the editors of the *Britannica,* would be up to the task of describing them. Those specially designed gadgets defy the most flamboyant imagination—but obviously they work. At sixty, having spent a life the like of which few humans have led, De Mille does not look a day older than forty-seven and has more vitality and energy than the average man of thirty. He thinks nothing of rowing for ten or twelve miles at a stretch and his idea of a pleasant walk is anywhere from five to twenty miles.

Invests Wisely

The clock strikes eight. His breakfast consumed and his newspapers read, De Mille is ready for action. He walks down the long glass-enclosed passageway briskly and bids a cheerful good morning to Gladys Rosson, a quiet and extremely efficient lady who has acted as his private secretary since 1915, and who smiles tolerantly whenever she hears outsiders say that her boss is hell on wheels. Not unlike all other people who know De Mille really well, she feels that at least ninety-five per cent of his fantastic outbursts is an "act."

C. B. settles at a huge desk and tackles his mail. It covers a great variety of subjects, mostly financial. One of the richest men in the industry, he has invested his money wisely. He owns real estate, has considerable holdings in oil companies, and until recently acted as vice-president of the Bank of America. "Acted" is right; he has never consented to be a dummy. The heads of the Bank of America discovered at the very outset of their relations with De Mille, that when he accepted the vice-presidency he meant that no one was to interfere with the running of the branch of the bank entrusted to him.

There is nothing la-di-da or eccentric about the way De Mille conducts his business affairs. He reaches clear-cut decisions and never postpones answering the letters from his partners, agents, and lawyers. When once in a blue moon he hesitates and asks Miss Rosson, "What do you think of it?" she knows better than to answer, "Well, Mr. De Mille, I guess—" Nothing irritates De Mille more than that "I guess" business. "I can guess myself!" he roars at the offending party. "I want your opinion. I don't give a damn about your guesses!"

It's eight thirty by now. Time to go to the studio. Before climbing into his car, a none too prepossessing affair the like of which he wouldn't dream of tolerating in even his least expensive picture, he casts an uneasy glance at the house across the street. W. C. Fields lives there, and De Mille has long since given up trying to analyze his neighbor's behavior. Why, for instance, should that man insist, this morning when it's raining cats and dogs, on sitting on his lawn, clad in silk pajamas and hiding under a tiny umbrella not large enough to protect even his nose?

Enter The Showman

Some students of the Hollywood scene claim Fields gets no thrill at all out of being drenched but that he cannot resist the temptation of sowing a few seeds of confusion in De Mille's orderly mind. Be that as it may, so far apart are the two men, physically, emotionally, mentally, that they should have been separated by the whole width of the African continent rather than by a narrow street. In his capacity as air warden of the district, De Mille is compelled once in a while to ring the bell of the Fields house and point out to its inhabitants that the alarm has sounded and that they must fill their bathtubs, turn out all lights, and so on. He confesses that he would just as soon endeavor to explain relativity to a herd of seals.

It's only a few miles from C. B.'s house to Paramount, but the man who alights at the studio gate ten minutes later has nothing in common with the man we watched dictating letters to Miss Rosson. Exit De Mille the financier. Enter De Mille the showman. His very appearance undergoes a drastic change. Those blue-gray eyes that conveyed kindness and shrewdness only ten short minutes before are throwing sparks of defiant impatience now. He runs, not walks, to his office on the lot. The heels of his high boots thud ominously, and the assistant who came to report on "work in progress" knows that he's in for a severe tongue-lashing.

Sam Wood, the man who achieved what amounts to immortality in Hollywood by directing *Goodbye Mr. Chips* and *Kitty Foyle*, used to work as De Mille's assistant years ago. He still shakes with laughter when he thinks of those early-morning conferences with his boss. He remembers that historic day when De Mille said to him, "Do you realize, Sam, that in our next scene we must have a leopard?"

"Oh, sure," replied Wood. "I thought of it last night and I got hold of a fine-looking stuffed one."

"A stuffed leopard!" cried De Mille. "A stuffed leopard in *my* picture!"

Three DeMilles, Agnes, Cecil, and Kathryn.

Sam Wood, who became one of Hollywood's top directors, started as assistant to C. B.

It was as if Wood had suggested to him that he should desecrate the flag or choke his mother. When De Mille finally regained his powers of speech, he said in a tone which one would order a sandwich from a very stupid waiter, "I want a three-year-old leopard—and not too spotted."

"A three-year-old leopard—not too spotted," repeated Wood. "Where do I find it, C. B.?"

"Mr. Wood," said De Mille sternly, "you seem to forget that you are the assistant director on this picture, not I. It's your business to know where to find a piece of stage property."

"Yes, sir," said Wood meekly.

Episode With Leopard

The people at the Los Angeles Zoo to whom he stated De Mille's specifications said that the only leopard they had for sale was nine years old and spotted as all hell.

"He'll do," decided Wood.

He telephoned De Mille and announced he had found just the thing.

"How old is it?" asked De Mille.

"They celebrated his third birthday last Tuesday," said Wood.

"How about spots?"

"C. B.," said Wood, "I never thought I'd live to see a leopard that had less spots than this one."

The transaction completed, Wood found himself in possession, but alas not in control, of a vicious-looking animal that seemed to hate all mammals, particularly those connected with the motion-picture industry. When the late Thomas Meighan, who was playing in the picture, took one look at the leopard, he locked himself in his dressing room and said he would not return to the set unless and until something was done to protect him against the attacks of that "foul beast."

"Mr. Wood," asked De Mille, "what do you propose to do about it? It's your job, you know. I handle the actors; my assistant is supposed to handle the minor details of the production."

"Yes, sir," said Wood. For a moment he toyed with the idea of giving up the motion-picture business and telling De Mille where he got off, but then he thought better of it. He was not going to admit defeat. Come hell or high water, he was going to prove to that blankety-blank leopard that the assistant director *was* in charge of all minor details of the production.

He went across the street to the studio's drugstore, and came back carrying a sponge and a huge bottle of chloroform. The first thing the leopard knew, he was asleep—sufficiently so to reassure Meighan.

Unfortunately for all parties concerned, however, De Mille was in an inventive mood that day. He was looking for a new camera angle and was not prepared to shoot the scene until he found one. The new camera angle was yet to be found when the leopard awoke, emitted one ferocious snarl, and leaped forward.

"Mr. Wood," cried De Mille, "I cannot tolerate this disturbance! Stop that cat at once!"

"Yes, sir," said Wood.

Two bottles of chloroform and several deep scratches later, he finally managed to prove to the cat that a leopard, while perhaps one of the kings of the jungle in Africa, was only a minor detail in Hollywood.

There was no Sam Wood around when De Mille was shooting *Cleopatra* with Claudette Colbert. When it came to the famous suicide scene, C. B.'s assistant frankly confessed that he was not up to the task of persuading Miss Colbert to handle the deadly asp.

"Very well," said the benevolent tyrant; "I'll do the persuading."

Passion For Realism

When the great moment arrived and Cleopatra was properly installed on the golden throne of the Pharaohs, De Mille walked straight up to her with a six-foot long live California king snake coiled around his right arm.

Warren William and Claudette Colbert in one of C. B.'s first epics, Cleopatra.

Behind his back in his left hand, he held the diminutive snake that was to enact the role of the asp.

"No, no, no!" shrieked Colbert, "I wouldn't dream of touching that horrible thing. I wouldn't do it for a billion dollars!"

"Then how about this one?" suggested De Mille, producing the little snake.

"Oh, that's different," cooed Colbert. "Why, this one is just a baby." And without further to-do she grabbed the little fellow out of De Mille's hand as if afraid that he might change his mind and insist on her handling the lengthy king snake.

Stars and assistant directors are not the only ones who suffer because of De Mille's passion for realistic touches and correct details. Adolph Zukor and Jesse L. Lasky, then the heads of Paramount, used to spend sleepless nights wondering what new extravagant request would be made by their prize director. Their fears were well founded. One day he would insist that an authentic set of armor had to be provided for each and every player appearing in *Joan the Woman*, a picture based on the life of Joan of Arc. The next day, with—out batting an eyelash, he would spend fifteen hundred dollars on a chinchilla-trimmed nightgown not even to be worn but simply dragged across the floor by Gloria Swanson in a short sequence in one of her films. When the New York office remonstrated with him about that particular expenditure and mentioned something about what their bankers would say, De Mille was genuinely surprised.

C. B. directs Gary Cooper in The Plainsman.

"Why," he said, "don't you realize that that fifteen-hundred-dollar nightgown would mean at least a hundred and fifty thousand dollars more in the box office?"

Amazingly enough, he was right. So great was the impression made by the nightgown on the housewives of America that several newspapers burst forth with indignant editorials about it and the picture grossed a quarter of a million more than was expected.

Careful Research

When a year later New York found out that the irrepressible C. B. was shopping for royal brocade, to the tune of two hundred dollars per yard, for the costumes to be used in his forthcoming picture, no one dared argue; but one brave soul did gather enough courage to ask, "How will the customers know if it's real brocade at two hundred dollars a yard or a cheap substitute at two dollars a yard?"

"Ah," smiled De Mille, "the customers won't know, but my actors and actresses will. Can you imagine a woman star wearing some three thousand dollars' worth of brocade on her person and not giving the best performance of her life? That's why I always use real orchids in my pictures. They cost seven fifty apiece, but they're worth it. It does something even to a dumb gal playing a bit when you hand her a corsage for which she knows the company paid thirty or forty dollars."

New York remained speechless. So, on top of everything, that man was having real orchids even for the extra players! And at forty dollars a corsage, too!

A master and a slave of detail, a hard-hitting perfectionist and a blue-eyed daydreamer,

DeMille hated yes men. "I want a man to disagree with me 60% of the time," he once said.

De Mille spends more time and money on research than any other producer or director under the sun. Prior to shooting *The Buccaneer,* a picture dealing with New Orleans during the War of 1812, he went all over Louisiana gathering books, diaries, photography, and so on. His files show that the sum of $110,000 was invested in that scientific expedition. By the time De Mille was ready to proceed with the picture itself, he could have written a twelve-volume treatise on New Orleans, Andrew Jackson and his generals, the fashions and the most popular dishes of 1812, and heaven only knows what else.

The people who imagined that they knew a thing or two about the War of 1812 and thus should be hired as technical advisers for *The Buccaneer* left C. B.'s presence shaking their heads in dismay.

"That man," muttered one of them, "is wasting his time and talents here in Hollywood. He ought to be teaching American history in Harvard or Princeton instead of monkeying with films."

Nothing pleases De Mille more than to be given the opportunity to catch the so-called experts in an error. He still chuckles when he recalls how, while conducting research for *Union Pacific,* he discovered that the famous phrase "Go West, young man, go West" had never been coined by Horace Greeley (who was credited with it for several generations) but was first written by an unsung editor of a humble weekly paper in Terre Haute, Indiana.

An Egyptian Prank

"They accuse me of inaccuracies," he says, banging the table with his fist, "but what would happen if I ever dared to put on the screen some of the things that actually happened in ancient times? Take, for instance, my picture *Cleopatra.* The critics said that mine was a Park Avenue Cleopatra. Poor lambs. If they'd only known what I found out about Cleopatra in the scripts of the period! Have you ever heard of the practical joke she played on Mark Antony when they went on a fishing cruise? Listen to this. She made one of her slaves dive in the river and attach a beautifully cooked fish to Antony's hook. I would have given my right arm to use that sequence in my picture, but how could I? Even the public would have said, 'Just another of De Mille's crazy tricks!' "

A money director par excellence, De Mille has long since become accustomed to being manhandled by critics and highbrows. His record speaks. It's an astonishing one. In his thirty years as director and producer he has turned out sixty-six pictures for which the public paid $200,000,000 at the box office and which grossed for Paramount alone the important sum of $55,000,000.

Recently, while both men were sitting in the projection room looking at the "dailies," De Mille jumped up, pointed a threatening finger at the screen, and yelled at the top of his voice, "This stinks! Stinks to high heaven. I'm ashamed of you, Rosson! My five-year-old grandson could take a better shot than that. Why, man, don't you realize—" And off he went.

When he was through, Rosson spoke up. "C. B., it so happens that I didn't take that shot. You did."

"It's a lie!" thundered De Mille. "Fancy *my* taking that shot. Why, it's preposterous!"

They summoned the cameraman. He looked up his records, and announced that the shot in question had in truth been taken by Cecil De Mille. The great man waved him aside impatiently.

"I don't give a damn who took it!" he shouted. "De Mille or Rosson or John Doe. It stinks to heaven, I'm telling you!"

Several weeks later, at the private preview of the finished picture, De Mille motioned to Art Rosson to stand up, and said, "Ladies and gentlemen, permit me to introduce to you Mr. Art Rosson, the man who does the work for which I take the credit."

Few Know C.B.

Supercolossal as De Mille's eccentricities are, there is a great deal of difference between him and the usual run of Hollywood dictators. He hates and despises yes men. Once upon a

Adolph Zukor (fourth from left), Paramount chief, threatened to scrap Ten Commandments *because of cost. When C.B. offered to buy it Zukor went ahead with the project.*

time a certain individual who thought he could get around any one by constantly saying "You're perfectly right. I agree with you 100 per cent," tried his technique on C. B. He got his walking papers twenty-four hours later. "I've no use for people who agree with me 100 per cent," explained De Mille. "What I am looking for is a guy who'll disagree with me at least 60 per cent."

He found such a guy in the person of Bill Pine. It is estimated that, year in and year out, Pine distinguished himself by disagreeing with his boss at least 75 per cent. This led to some of the most spectacular fights in De Mille's career. He would denounce Pine vehemently in front of the company; he would all but wipe his boots on his daring associate. Then he would wind up by following Pine's advice. Very early in their association Pine understood that there is only one thing that De Mille will not stand for. In no circumstances should any one ever tell him that something he wanted to do was impossible. "What do you mean, impossible?" De Mille would yell. "Nothing is impossible on my lot! You forget that you're talking to the man who opened and closed the Red Sea."

Stormy as De Mille's dealings are with his associates, writers, actors, actresses, art directors, and cameramen, he seems to be guided by a sound principle. In his case, confidence inspires affection and not the other way around. His fondness for Gary Cooper verges on adoration; but there is an excellent reason for it. It so happens that he trusts Cooper implicitly and knows that he can always depend on him to deliver the best possible performance.

Nothing Impossible

When he was right in the middle of working on *The Ten Commandments*, the Paramount bookkeepers discovered that they had made a slight miscalculation; the epic would cost the company $400,000 more than the budget indicated. Adolph Zukor threw up his hands and said that enough was enough—De Mille had to be stopped. It was better, thought Mr. Zukor, to abandon the whole project than to let him wreck the company.

De Mille refused to argue. He took off his polo shirt, breeches, and high boots, put on a lounge suit befitting Cecil B. De Mille the financier, and went to see his lawyer, Neil McCarthy.

"Neil," he said to him, "I want you to leave for New York at once. I want to buy *The Ten Commandments* from Paramount and finish and release the picture on my own. I agree in advance to pay whatever price Zukor considers fair." McCarthy took the first train for New York and submitted De Mille's offer to Zukor.

"Are you prepared to pay us one million dollars?" asked Zukor, fully aware of the fact that De Mille did not have that much cash on hand.

"Yes," replied McCarthy, "provided you give us seventy-two hours to raise the money."

"It's a deal," said Zukor.

McCarthy went to his hotel, got A. P. Giannini, head of the Bank of America, on the long-distance telephone, and explained his predicament. The banker listened to him in silence, then asked just one question.

"Does C. B. believe that the picture will make money?"

"He does."

"You'll have the million dollars. I'll confirm it by wire right away."

When Zukor read Giannini's telegram, he asked McCarthy to leave it with him for a few hours. That afternoon Paramount announced that its board of directors had decided to go ahead with *The Ten Commandments*.

"But you can't do it," protested McCarthy. "You've agreed to sell the picture to De Mille."

"My dear man," said Zukor, with a twinkle in his eye, "do you think I'm crazy? If it's good enough for the Bank of America, it's certainly good enough for my bankers."

It is a matter of record that *The Ten Commandments* made more money for Paramount than any other picture produced by that company.

Who Runs DeMille?

Partly because of his ability to combine the financial practices of a drunken sailor with the judgment of a banker, partly because of his unpredictable reactions and a thoroughly uncontrollable temper, De Mille is a puzzle—and

Adolph Zukor helps celebrate C. B.'s birthday.

a considerable headache—to ninety-nine per cent of the men and women in the industry. This is not surprising, because his is the best known name and the least known personality in Hollywood. Not a joiner (he doesn't play golf and doesn't belong to any clubs), not an invitation-seeker, De Mille managed to spend thirty years in a town where everybody knows everybody else, and where most of the people get into one another's hair, without having acquired any friends or enemies to speak of. Those few individuals who met him years and years ago (his lawyer McCarthy, his scenarist Jeanie Macpherson, his cutter Anne Bauchens, his former associate producer Bill Pine, and his former assistant Mitchell Leisen) are about the only ones who need no X-rays to learn what makes him run.

They know him as one knows one's favorite bed slippers. Nothing he says, does, or undertakes ever surprises them. When De Mille picks up the phone, calls Leisen, and barks, "Mitch, I want you to take a test for me," Leisen never bothers to explain that it has been years since he graduated from C. B.'s assistant into a big director in his own right. He merely says, "Certainly, C. B.," and goes ahead and takes the test. When De Mille yells at Bill Pine and reprimands him for something which he considers "utterly inexcusable and almost criminal," Pine listens patiently and promises he will try to mend his ways. Like Leisen, Pine is not working for De Mille any more; and like Leisen, he too realizes that once a De Mille slave always a De Mille slave.

Art Rosson, a mild-mannered man who is in charge of De Mille's so-called second unit (a unit that takes outdoor shots, battle scenes, and the like while the master is working in the studio), has been with De Mille a great many years, and he's still convinced that were he to live to be as old as Methuselah, even then he would never be able to shoot a scene in a way that would please his boss.

History has never known a tyrant who was strong enough not to be won over and mastered by some one, usually a person who chose to remain behind the scenes. Cecil B. De Mille is no exception to the rule. He may have opened and closed the Red Sea, and he may have forced the tempestuous Paulette Goddard to rehearse sixteen times the scene in which she is soundly spanked by four husky Northwest Mounted policemen, but he ceases to be the führer and turns into a piece of putty when it comes to matching wits with his seven-year-old granddaughter, Cecilia Harper. It is this little red-haired girl who really runs the great Mr. De Mille. What she says goes, at least in their household.

One evening a few months ago, on his return home after a hard day at the studio, De Mille was notified that Cecilia had refused to say her prayers. Her mother pleaded with her, but she said no, she was too tired, and besides she just didn't believe in saying prayers. "I'll have a talk with her," promised C. B. He did, but failed to sway the rebel.

"I'm too tired," she kept repeating.

"All right, darling," he compromised. "I'll tell you what I'll do. I'll say your prayers for you."

It is quite possible that the picture of an elderly man kneeling by the bedside of a child struck him as being an excellent idea for a touching closeup. Be that as it may, he began reciting the prayer. Cecilia listened patiently at first; but when he reached the middle, she cut him short.

"This is Cecil B. De Mille saying good night from Hollywood, California," she announced, yawning lustily.

C. B. with granddaughter Cecilia.

The Battle of Detroit

by Frederick L. Collins

Early in 1942 Fred L. Collins looked for an answer to the question, "Why wasn't the big armament push possible earlier?" Here is what he found.

"Don't send me men, send me equipment," said John Gort, commander of the British Expeditionary Forces just before the ill-fated battle of Dunkirk. Realizing that it took material as well as men to win wars, the U.S. began "turning it out." (Above) The B-24 plant at Willow Run; (middle) the Ford tank assembly line in Detroit; (below) the Dodge Motor Company manufactures trucks and weapons carriers.

The Battle of the Pacific has been added to the Battle of the Atlantic. Battles are so big these days that we do not call them after harbors or capes or fields or towns, as we did in the legendary days of Trafalgar and Waterloo. We call them after oceans or countries.

The Battle of France. That shook the world. The Battle of Britain. That seemed like the end of that shaken world. The Battle of Russia. Who knows how that may turn out?

But when history is written—and it *will* be written in spite of Nazi edicts against free speech, free writing, and free brains—none of these conflicts will be hailed "the greatest battle of the greatest war."

The greatest battle, because it must inevitably be the decisive battle, is the Battle of Detroit.

Detroit, as no American needs to be told, is a generic term for Flint and Lansing, Dearborn and Ypsilanti, Indianapolis and South Bend, Dayton and Toledo, Bridgeport and Hartford, San Diego and Inglewood—wherever America is arming.

And why is it the greatest battle? That's easy. What did Gort say before Dunkirk, Gort the heroic commander of the ill-fated B. E. F.?

"Don't send me men. Send me equipment!"

What did poor little bewildered Paul Reynaud say when he appealed to the President in France's extremity?

"Send us clouds of planes."

Of course Britain didn't have the equipment to send Gort, America didn't have the clouds of planes to send Reynaud—so there was Dunkirk and there was France. But that does not alter the fact that man power on the field of battle is the least of our worries in the fight against Hitler.

In World War I, it took an average of two and a half to three men behind the lines to keep one combat soldier supplied. In World War II, the ratio is something like seventeen or eighteen to one.

This is the war of the invisible man. Thousands of Frenchmen defending the Maginot Line never saw a German soldier. All they saw were bomber planes and tanks. Men used to carry weapons; now weapons carry men.

In short, this war must be won, as we still so quaintly say, "at the lathe."

But if all this is true—and it is true—and if those in authority realize it—and they do—why has it taken so long to get that lathe to turning?

Why aren't we getting results?

Why aren't we producing clouds of planes, fleets of tanks?

Or are we?

I don't know any question more important to you, Mr. and Mrs. Reader.

You are buying guns, shells, tanks, bombers—forty to sixty billion dollars' worth of them. You'll probably buy a hundred billion dollars' worth before long. You are entitled to know whether the defense drive is really a drive or just a putt.

To change the figure and to put the case more specifically, you are entitled to know why the defense program has been, so far, a trickle instead of a flood, and when, if ever, it is going to be a flood.

Why Not Earlier?

Answering the first part of that question first, there are many explanations, of which you have heard plenty and then some. True, too, so far as they go:

Headline-hunting senatorial Neros fiddling with syntax while freedom burned.

Brass-hat brass-hattedness—which is another phrase for mental inflexibility—taking six months to make up its mind about a problem which the average American executive would have decided before lunch.

Labor troubles. A twenty-eight-day soft-coal strike, translated into terms of lost steel production, cost the United States fourteen first-class battleships. No naval engagement in history has inflicted such devastation on a patriotic people.

Sure, all that stuff is true. At times it has been important. Perhaps it is nothing more than we should expect from a non-war-minded nation forced suddenly to get war-minded. But we are fed up with these explanations. They are, we say, Washington stuff—all wrapped up in SPABS, OEMS, OMPS, OPAS, and what have you—Washington, where not much can be done, and where, apparently, so disappointingly little is being done.

Billboards promoted war production—men were needed to build planes, tanks, ships.

We have heard too much from Washington. We have heard too little from Detroit.

And that is why I pulled on my old World War I pants—without all those silly leather gaiters, of course—and went out as a roving war correspondent to cover the American front. And I have covered it. Not all of it, of course, for it is as long as the nation is wide, but plenty.

I have seen America arming.

I have seen great automobile factories turning out 75-millimeter and 105-millimeter shells by mass production at a rate never dreamed of by Mars or Vulcan, Hitler or Goring; great spark-plug factories, twelve months ahead of schedule, turning out machine guns that fire faster and farther than any such gun before known.

I have seen 12,000 men—who were a few months ago unemployed preachers, barbers, farm hands, and haberdashers—working in a giant factory—which only a few months ago was a wind-swept cornfield—making 1,000 airplane engines a month for an exclusively American model which weighs less and generates more horsepower per pound than any airplane engine Hitler even dreamed about.

I have seen twenty-eight-ton tanks rolling off assembly lines the way tin Lizzies used to roll—only they are *not* tin, but tougher steel than Nazi Germany knows how to make; and the first Nazi German that runs up against them will find out they are not Lizzies—that is, he will find out if he can catch up with them, because these American tanks travel three times as fast as Hitler's fastest tank.

I have seen the largest bomber factory in the world rising on a thousand acres—which a few months ago was an age-old forest—into which thousands of small pieces of steel and aluminum and magnesium are now pouring, and out of which, at the far end of the world's longest assembly line, will shortly pour complete air fortresses, giant tanks of the air, which will streak down a mile-long runway and hop off for Europe.

I have seen—but what's the use? You can't put a nation's greatest effort, a world's biggest business, into a paragraph. And, besides, I can hear you saying:

"If all this is possible now, why wasn't it possible six months ago?"

It was.

Need Special Facilities

Not all, but most of the defense material which is being shipped today could have been shipped in the same quantity six months ago. Guns, for example, could have been made on the old-fashioned small-production basis, using machinery already in possession of the government, some of it twenty-five years old, some of it seventy years old.

By sticking to these methods, playing safe, and dodging criticism, defense industries could have gotten about as far as they have gotten—in actual production, I mean—and gotten there a whole lot sooner. But that is as far as they could have gotten, substantially as far as they ever would get, by such outdated procedure—and that wouldn't be far enough to lick Hitler or even annoy him.

To adopt such a course would have been to admit at the start that we could not hope to match the speed of Nazi production, to say nothing of topping it. And that admission, as we have seen, would be fatal. For victory in this war, to paraphrase the remarks of a famous American general, goes to the side that has the "mostest" equipment and gets there "fustest."

One of our greatest American motor makers, now involuntarily turned munitions maker, sums it up more grammatically in a sentence. "It is a race in tonnage 'produced' and tonnage 'delivered' on the heads of the enemy."

Obviously it would be impossible to win that race by employing production methods which the enemy had himself long since abandoned!

The alternative—which the men who are fighting the Battle of Detroit courageously took, although they knew full well that it would subject them in the beginning to harshest criticism—was to go about the laborious business of designing tools, manufacturing machinery, and constructing plants which would ultimately put the manufacture of guns and shells and tanks and bombers on the same mass-production basis on which the manufacture of automobiles has been these many years.

New Kinds Of Work

That took time.

As one motor maker put it: "The heart of mass production is coordination and exactness, reaching back through a thousand preparatory steps. Even though the automobile industry has over four decades of experience in making annual model changes, a full year's intensive work is essential between the development of new designs and the production of new models."

And these aren't just new models of automobiles that are now pouring off America's assembly lines. They aren't merely alterations of existing things. They are new things, in many cases things the present makers never saw before, and, until a few months ago, couldn't have called by name, let alone build and train others to build.

"More than 70 per cent of the $1,200,000,000 in defense obligations assumed or under negotiation by General Motors," said Chairman Alfred P. Sloan, Jr., "are for products other than those normally manufactured by the corporation's divisions, and only about 10 per cent are within the normal area of the automotive industry. To produce these highly specialized types of defense materials requires, of course, special facilities, including specifically designed machines and tools and in many instances completely new plants. In this connection, General Motors has under construction or already completed fourteen such new plants, as well as thirteen important plant expansions. In addition, twenty-six existing buildings have been reequipped with machinery for defense production."

When Packard took on the big job of producing 9,000 Rolls-Royce liquid-cooled engines, it was found that only 3 per cent of its regular automotive equipment could be adapted and

Before U.S. entry into the war F.D.R. okays A.F. of L. poster promoting Defense Bonds.

Henry Ford (l) and Charles A. Lindbergh. Lindbergh went to work in Ford's B-24 Liberator Bomber plant as consultant for aeronautical and engineering research.

re-tooled to make aircraft engines. Consequently Packard was forced to order more than 3,000 new tools and to wait for these and for the manufacture of other equipment before starting actual production.

This was only half the Packard problem. Seventeen thousand workers had to be recruited and trained to operate the new machines. In fact, here and everywhere throughout the defense effort the training of the seventeen or eighteen industrial soldiers needed to keep one combat soldier in action has been the biggest problem the new munitions makers have had.

Take the AC spark-plug factory in Flint: The day before the management was told that henceforth they would be machine-gun manufacturers, only two men in the entire plant had ever seen a machine gun closer than a Warner Brothers movie. AC, therefore, had to begin its training system from scratch, with a nucleus of eight experienced foremen from its regular staff, who undertook to learn, and did learn, how to make the guns themselves. Then each of these eight took on ten other candidates for foremen's jobs and taught them what they had just learned. In this way a staff of some eighty foremen and assistant foremen were assembled.

The next step was to obtain from the Flint public schools—which had meantime set up two shifts of night courses in machine-shop work—partially trained boys and young men who could be developed into operators capable of running such machines as require a considerable amount of manual skill. Having built strongly from the top down, the AC people then took on unskilled laborers, about 40 per cent of them girls, who could be taught a few simple movements of routine production work. By this painstaking method, together with many revolutionary improvements worked out by its engineers, AC was able to go into production one year before the date it had promised and is still one year ahead of schedule.

I have talked with these men—the bosses, the foremen, the men on the assembly line—not just in Flint but all around the circuit, and I have to report that the spirit, without which these miracles would not be possible, is uniformly fine. Especially is this true of the men who have entered defense service from other lines of work. Here are three typical expressions gathered, as it happens, from the Olds Forge plant in Lansing:

"I ran a grocery store in Diamondale. Still got an interest in it, as a matter of fact. But here I've learned to run a machine which notches the end of the shell, and believe me it's mighty important, 'cause that's where the cap is fastened on. I can tell you there's much less grief in this job than in running a grocery store!"

"I'm twenty-nine and I've got three kids. I drove a cab in Lansing for nearly five years and I used to work twelve hours a day and six days a week doing it. I've learned to operate a vertical lathe on this job. I like it swell and I haven't missed a day yet."

"I was a barber for thirteen years and ran a tailor ship on the side. In the three months I've been here I've learned to run this hydraulic-press banding machine. And I've sure found out that the saying 'as fine as a hair' doesn't mean a thing compared with the measurements we've got to keep to on these shells. This beats barbering and tailoring all out!"

Defense Different

No matter how good the spirit, however, no matter how resourceful the management, and no matter how ingenious the engineering, we must not lose sight of the fact that these defense workers, from top to bottom, are doing new jobs about which most of them had never even heard twelve months ago. They must be given time to master those jobs.

"Bedroom" for bomber pilots at Ford aeronautical plant houses over 1,300 army cots.

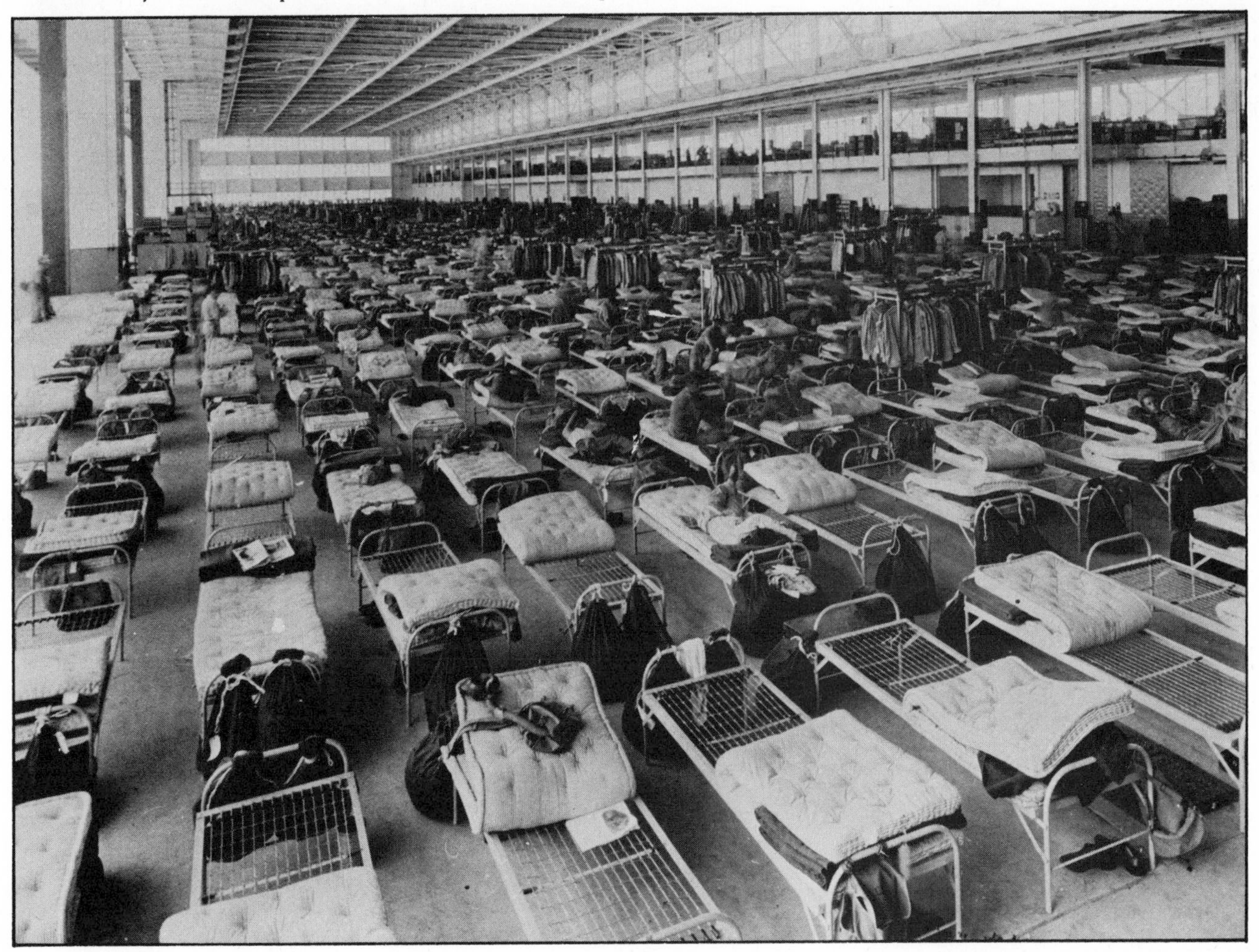

Former automobile plant was turned into 20mm machine gun factory during production drive.

In other words, machine guns aren't spark plugs, bombers aren't automobiles. Tools that will make one won't make the other. New tools must be designed, new machines manufactured, new processes evolved. Most important of all, men must be trained to new jobs. All this is necessary before mass production on a super-Hitler basis is begun.

Perhaps you know all this. But I didn't—until I went out where the work begins—and I think there are a lot of other good American citizens just as dumb as I was about these things. They should be told. They are counting on the Battle of Detroit as a main line of defense in today's war. They should know.

I put this phase of the matter up to one of the big generals on the Detroit front, a top production man, and this is what he said:

"There is a lack of national understanding (and it exists in fairly high places) of what it takes to bridge the difference between material 'on order' and material 'on hand.' There are weeks', months', often many months', difference between the two. With the exception of military trucks, all defense material differs radically, more or less—mostly more—from the materials used currently in mass production. These materials for defense are more highly stressed and must be much more accurately made. Broadly speaking, they have not been designed with mass production in view at all."

President C. E. Wilson of General Motors backed up that statement with a graphic example when he pointed out that the cost of automobiles at wholesale is less than twenty-five cents a pound, whereas the cost of airplanes and aviation engines is five to ten dollars a pound.

"Generally speaking," continued my production man, "the public thinks there is little difference between an automobile engine and an aircraft engine, and this is not difficult to understand. They are both gasoline engines, aren't they? If you are set up to build large quantities of the automobile engine, you should be able to switch to quantity production of the airplane engine immediately. Well, both are engines, both use gasoline, both are four-cycle; but when this has been said you are well on the way to exhausting the points of similarity."

As a matter of fact, if an aviation engine were to be made of the same materials and in the same manner as an automobile engine, it would weigh more than the whole airplane!

I emphasize this matter of the difference between an automobile engine and an aviation engine, because so many really intelligent people still cling to the notion that planes are driven by the same kinds of mechanism that automobiles are, and should be turned out by the same machinery and at the same rate.

Well enough meaning labor leaders, who rush into print with statements that the defense program has lagged because all machines in automobile factories aren't working full time, suffer from this delusion. Regulation automobile machines are idle half the time, it is true, but that is because the government, in the interest of preserving necessary materials for national defense, has cut down the production of automobiles by approximately 50 per cent.

If there is *one* idle machine in the automobile industry that *can* make defense material and *isn't*, finder will please notify Messrs. Ford, Keller, Sloan, *et al.*, and receive reward!

No, defense is not a part-time, by-product, warmed-over job. It is brand new: something Americans didn't know anything about, weren't prepared to do, had to learn, like a trade.

And it isn't as if there was just one new trade to be learned.

General Motors, for example, is working on several hundred different war products in sixty plants scattered over thirty-five cities. I won't burden you with the list, but if I were to do so, you would see at once that getting ready to deliver on these new and widely different products is like starting new businesses, very complicated businesses, much bigger businesses than even the automobile industry has ever envisaged.

It's big business—the biggest ever attempted in the history of man.

And in addition to all the special factors

Auto parts plant turns out 155 mm shells.

This "Blitz Buggy" is headed for France.

we have enumerated, which make it necessary for defense industries to go slow at first in order to be able to go fast later, there is the usual tedious period which precedes any major change in mass prodiction. This period is known in the automobile business as "tooling up."

Moreover, this tooling-up process is not confined to the big concerns with which the government has contracted for mass production. No automobile manufacturer, not even Mr. Ford, makes all the parts which enter into the finished automobile. General Motors, for example, does business with some 10,000 "suppliers" scattered all over the country, on whom they know they can rely for special skills in the making of certain parts. For example, one item that a big company requires consists of 125 parts, 122 of which are made outside the company's own plants.

So the process of alteration and replacement and training which we have seen going on in the big plants on a large scale must also occur in these hundreds of small plants—and is occurring, but with much travail, because it is harder for the little fellow, with fewer engineering and management resources, to change over.

Several times in these paragraphs we have had occasion to mention machine tools, a subject with which most of us are very little familiar. We all know about the assembly lines, the finished product, but we have given little thought to how the pieces of metal which are fitted on the assembly into their proper places get the way they are: cut, drilled, bored, ground, made to fit. That is the work of the machine tools.

Preliminary Work

Now, in switching from peacetime work to wartime work, the making of every machine tool becomes a custom job, and a big one, too. Don't be misled by the word "tool." The ones I am referring to are no hammers or screw drivers. A riveter with a squeezing pressure of 100,000 pounds to the square inch is a tool, and it may weigh at least four tons.

Before manufacture on these giants can begin, reams of blueprint paper must be consumed by designers and engineers. Did I say reams? The story in Detroit is that it took 186 pounds of blueprints to produce the first American tank!

That may be an exaggeration, but this I know to be true: in one factory alone, 62,000 man hours of work were required to turn out 8,000 tool drawings, and another 231,000 man hours of work went into the making of these tools—jigs, fixtures, and gauges; then all this new machinery had to be installed and men taught to operate it before work on actual defense material could begin.

This, I submit, is the kind of job which requires expert treatment, and it is getting it from the men who are the very best of their very good kind. But not even the greatest engineering and manufacturing geniuses can eliminate altogether the element of time. As Mr. Knudsen points out, although we have the greatest doctors in the world and the finest hospitals, it still takes nine months to make a baby.

All of which is by way of answering the first question on everybody's lips: "Why has it taken so long?" Now the time has come to answer the next question: "What have we got, now that we've got it?"

That's easy. The nine months of defense gestation have passed.

Come out with me to Detroit and see the baby!

This plant in Detroit turned out tanks by the thousands—they helped win the war.

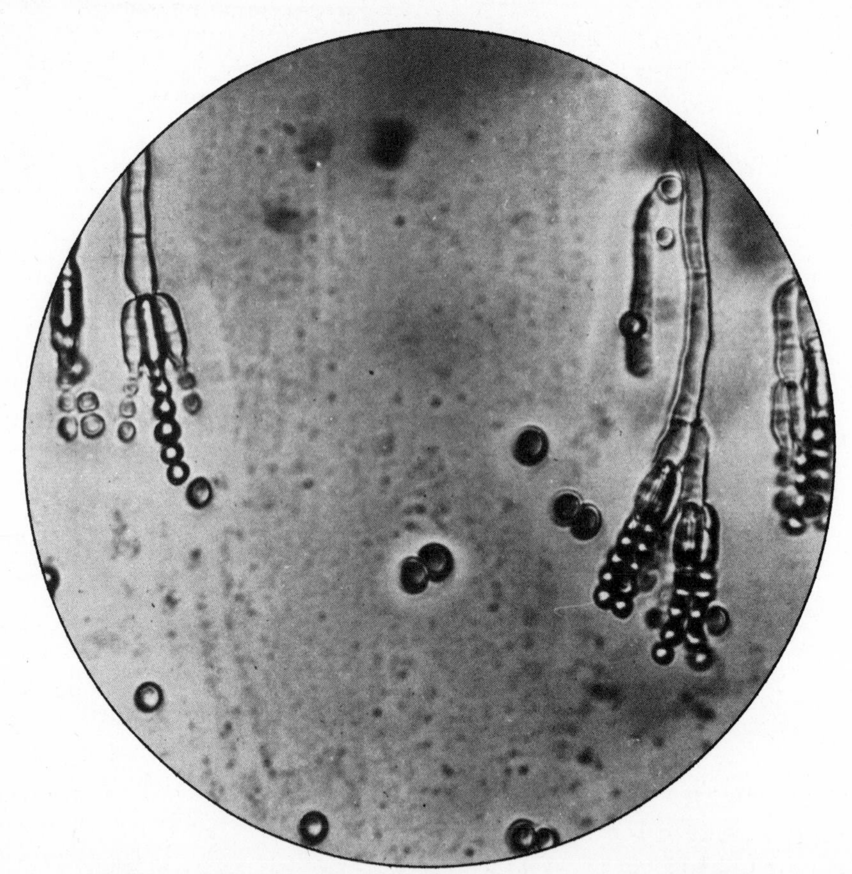

Penicillin-Medicine's Newest Miracle

by Antony Wymark

Penicillin's value was proved in 1942, but available supplies were ear-marked for the military. In 1943 Anthony Wymork described some of the difficulties in its general use.

On the night of November 28, 1942, fire swept a Boston night club, leaving in its wake a holocaust of death and destruction. Smoke, flames, and the boots of a panicking crowd brought the death toll to near 500. After sorting the injured from the dead and the dying, the doctors at the Boston City and Massachusetts General hospitals were faced with a deluge of casualties such as is seldom seen outside military hospitals. It was a grim and heartbreaking situation that called for extraordinary measures.

Action came fast. Long-distance wires hummed with the interchange of official O. K.'s and in Rahway, New Jersey, an unpretentious coupé headed silently into the night from the chemical research laboratories of Merck & Co., Inc. As the gates of the great factory clanged to behind it, a police escort swung into line and with sirens screaming the convoy headed northward. At state boundaries fresh relays of police took over.

Before dawn the procession had arrived at the gates of the Massachusetts General Hospital, the driver of the coupe worn and red-eyed from strain. Treating them as gingerly as if they were concentrated dynamite, he handed over to the waiting physicians an arm-load of innocent-looking packages. The doctors gazed curiously as, with a touch almost of reverence, they extracted the glass ampules from the boxes.

So this was penicillin—an uninteresting-looking brown powder that sluiced around in its glass container like sand in an egg-timer. This was the miracle drug that many believed would make the sulfa drugs appear as out-moded as the horse and buggy. Now it was to be put to the test on the burned patients in the wards. Deliberately the doctors chose the most severely injured. Over burned surfaces and into veins they poured the solution which they made from the brown powder.

Secrecy Broken

The results they obtained were closely guarded secrets, for Washington wanted to keep penicillin as hush-hush as the plans for a second front. But medical big-wigs, the men charged with the responsibility of advising the Army's Surgeon General, slipped into Boston quietly and, after reviewing the cases, stepped into their Pullmans nodding encouragingly to one another. Donald Robertson, brilliant bearded expert from the Merck Company, surveyed the patients with critical eyes and fingered his Vandyke approvingly. Penicillin, the most breath-taking medical discovery of the twentieth century, had arrived.

That was eight months ago. Since then, penicillin has pitted its mettle against the most hideous and virulent forms of bacterial disease that medical specialists could find. In peace-time the results would have been blazoned across the pages of the medical journals, but for reasons connected with the war the news has been circulated only among a small group of the nation's top-notch specialists. Now the secret has become too big to be any longer a secret, and Washington has broken its silence and announced publicly that the drug is being used in Army and Navy hospitals.

Behind penicillin lies a story of "blood, sweat, and tears" that ranges from a London hospital to the Mayo Clinic, from the halls of Oxford University to the conference rooms of Washington's office of Scientific Research and Development.

Penicillin received its first great test, not under battle conditions in Europe or the Pacific, but right here in this country in September of 1942 after a holocaust at the Cocoanut Grove in Boston (top) left a deluge of casualties in its wake. Penicillin did the job. Later it was flown to all theaters of war where it kept G.I.s alive.

It was in 1929, while Hitler was still biting his nails over the problem of gaining power, that Professor Alexander Fleming, as he pottered about his laboratory in a London hospital, first stumbled across the stuff. In the course of some routine studies he had left lying exposed on the laboratory bench a number of culture plates, shallow glass dishes smeared thinly with the jellylike food on which bacteria thrive. Germs from the atmosphere had settled on the plates and reproduced themselves profilically until now the jelly was freckled with bacterial colonies.

As the professor scanned these plates, his eye was attracted to one particular point where a fluffy kind of fungus, not unlike the mold which forms on stale bread, dominated the other clumps of bacteria. What stirred his curiosity was the strange fact that the bacterial colonies, jostling one another as they were for room, maintained a respectful distance between themselves and this fungus. It is common knowledge among scientists that a great many forms of microscopic life turn out poisons. It seemed to Fleming, as he held the culture plate up to the light, a fairly safe bet that this mold was maintaining its aloofness by means of a moat of liquid poison.

A surgeon as well as a bacteriologist, Fleming was a germ hater, and if this fungus could teach him how to poison his lifelong enemies he was willing to learn.

Alexander Fleming, discoverer of penicillin.

The first thing he had to do was to coax his precious fungus to continue living. After experimenting with a variety of foods, he discovered that the mold thrived when planted in common meat broth and poured out bacterial poison as fast as Kaiser turns out freighters.

From there Fleming went ahead rapidly. Pausing just long enough to christen his poison penicillin, he set to work to show which bacteria it kills and which it cannot touch. He devised methods of measuring its power and even tried it on a few ulcer cases in human beings, but the thing which would have been his crowning achievement he failed to do. Pencillin was stuck fast in the broth into which the mold spewed it, and try as he would he could not extract it. Pouring the poison-containing broth itself into his patients' veins was fraught with danger. Penicillin was as useless as a panzer division engulfed in a quagmire.

For more than a decade neither Fleming nor any one else took pains to retrieve the poison from the broth. Then a quiet spoken group of scientists, headed by Oxford University's brilliant Australian-trained professor of pathology Howard Florey—and backed by a grant from the Rockefeller Foundation—accomplished as a team what Fleming had failed to do alone. Penicillin, the wonder drug, a dirty brown powder, was snared by a simple extraction process that Fleming had overlooked.

It took no more than a few preliminary experiments to provide some hint of what the new drug could do to disease germs. Taken straight, it was just stark sudden death to them. Greatly diluted, it completely paralyzed their growth. Animals that had been inoculated with many times the ordinarily fatal dose of virulent disease germs recovered when they received injections of the drug. The controls, those animals which had received the germs

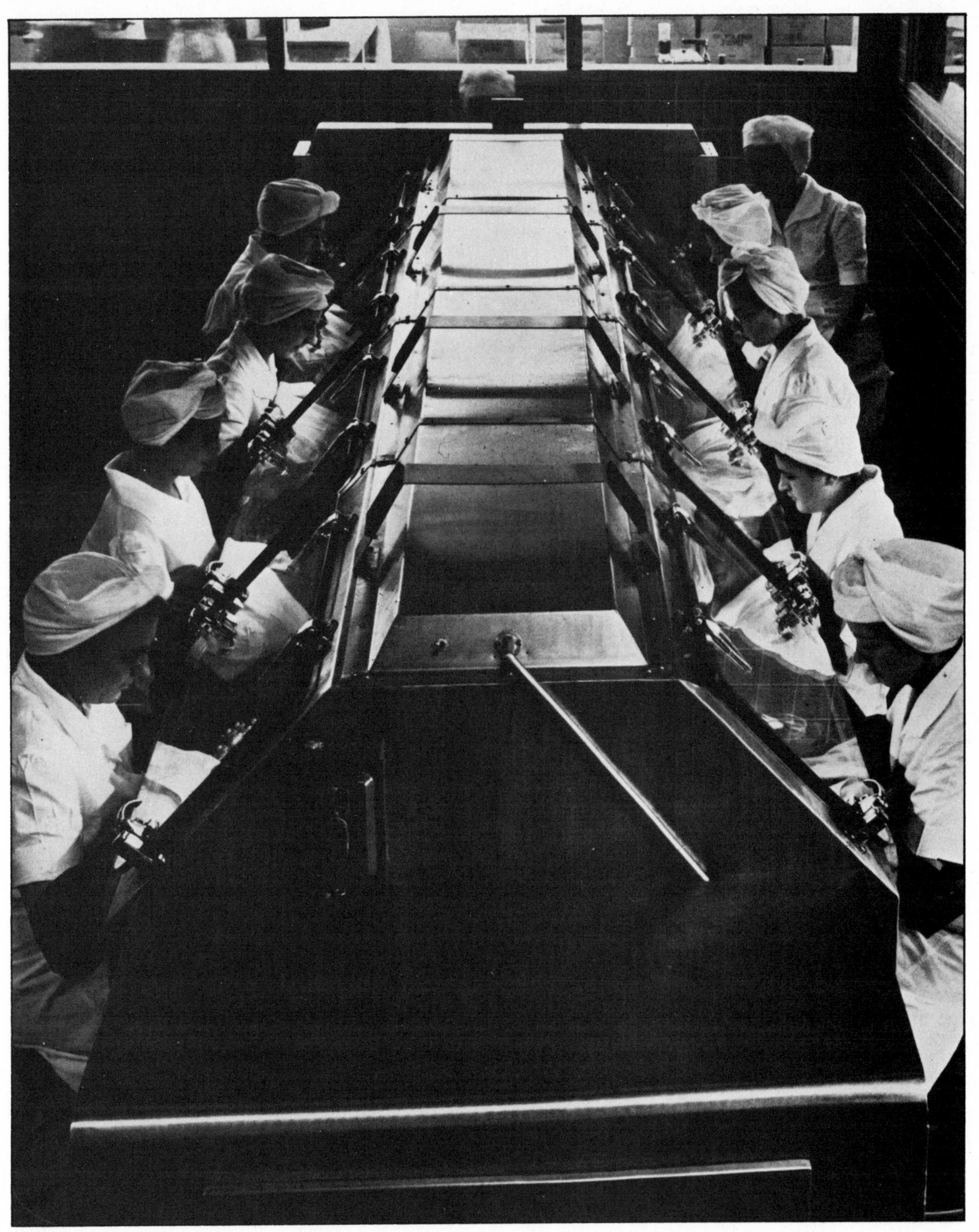

Workers at Merck, Inc., New Jersey ready penicillin for shipment to Cocoanut Grove victims.

but not the drug, rolled over on their backs and died before they knew what had hit them.

Can't Hurry Fungus

Clearly, here was a drug that was crying to high heaven for testing in human disease. There was just one fly in the ointment. The supply depended on a common fungus which refused to be hurried. To obtain the material in anything like reasonable quantities, the scientists needed to grow the mold on a far more extensive scale than their facilities would permit. Just as the outlook seemed blackest, inspiration struck them. Penicillin, they knew, is excreted in the urine. If they could only collect the urine from their patients, the drug could be recovered and after purification administered over and over again. Not all of it could be regained in this way, to be sure, but perhaps enough to see them through.

Their problem, at least for a preliminary trial, seemed to be solved. The first patient was a middle-aged policeman who had contracted blood poisoning from a neglected sore at the corner of his mouth. His body was covered with abscesses. A solution of penicillin was injected into his veins every three hours. The effect was electrifying. Within a day the patient looked and felt better, and, most astonishing of all, the abscesses were drying up. After five days the temperature became normal and the patient seemed on the road to recovery.

Then came tragedy. The supply of penicillin petered out. For ten days longer the patient held his own before the infection with regathered strength commenced its final assault on his weakened body. The blow was heartbreaking, but with stony determination the research workers set out to build up their miserably small stock of the drug. Over months, by dint of miserly hoarding, they were able to treat several more patients, all of them near death, their infections unresponsive to the sulfa drugs. Among them was a boy with a virulent blood poisoning arising from an abscess of the thigh bone complicated by inflammation of the kidneys. By dripping penicillin into his veins continuously, not only was his life saved but he was given back the use of the limb which no one had even dared hope might be useful again.

In other cases improvement was even more startling, but shortage of the drug hung always like a specter over every patient. Each case was a race against time, a race against the moment when the tiny allotment of penicillin would be exhausted. Even with pitifully inadequate doses the patients rallied, came tantalizingly close to recovery, and then, as supplies failed, slid slowly back, their unaided defenses crumbling before the invading bacteria.

Scientists, doctors above all, are not given to emotional display, but here was a situation to "try men's souls." Stolid and unemotional as they were on the surface, there burned within these scientific workers a fervent conviction that they had scratched only the surface possibilities of penicillin, that the latent power of the drug would revolutionize the practice of medicine. Between conviction and proof lay only one obstacle—lack of supplies. Enlargement of the production facilities was all but impossible. In that summer of 1941 Britain was still grasping desperately for every material which would cure the anemia caused by appeasement. Metals were going into Lancasters, not laboratories. The feeble voices that they could raise in Oxford would have been drowned in the general cry for guns long before they reached Whitehall. So Florey accepted the invitation of the Rockefeller Foundation to visit America.

Miracle Under Wraps

On his flying visit he found little difficulty in working up the enthusiasm of American scientists to fever pitch, but more difficult was the task of persuading potential manufacturers to sink hundreds of thousands of dollars in equipment devoted to turning out a product which might still prove to be only a flash-in-the-pan remedy. Yet by the time he returned to England he had in his briefcase assurances of production in this country of at least sufficient quantities to prove whether penicillin was a miracle or merely a mirage. To make sure there would be no dawdling, his crack production man stayed on with the Merck Company to teach the personnel how to speed the stuff along. Slowly the wheels of American

Alexander Fleming examines penicillin slide in Peoria, Illinois research lab where U.S. scientists helped develop drug. (Below) Penicillin is introduced to U.S. Army.

industry began to turn, but scarecly had production groped its way cautiously forward to pilot-plant scale when the United States went into the war.

From that moment secrecy wrapped penicillin like a shroud. The drug had become doubly precious, and the government clamped a demanding hand over all supplies. Research had to be speeded up. If penicillin turned out to be the magic healer that Florey claimed, the armed forces wanted it, and would brook no delay in getting it. To make sure that supplies went only to first-class research men, Dr. Chester Keefer, noted Boston specialist, was appointed to supervise the distribution for human trials.

All but top-notch specialists who could be relied upon to do a good job had to be turned down politely but firmly. As each case was treated, comprehensive reports were turned in to the newly appointed research boss. So far these reports have remained confidential, but it is common talk among the higher-ups of the medical world that before the onslaught of the drug pneumonia dissolves like a bad dream, the deep-set bone abscesses of osteomyelitis melt and heal, that even the almost invariably fatal blood poisoning with the dread staphylococcal germs is forced to yield.

Yet, despite the secrecy, details of a few cases have come to light. One such which came into Rochester's Mayo Clinic illustrates the strangle hold with which penicillin chokes the life out of disease germs. The patient, a man in his early thirties, had a spreading carbuncle involving the nose and eyelids, the so-called "danger area" of the face. Sepsis was creeping along the orbit, slowly squeezing the eye from the socket and threatening at any moment to invade the brain. After thirty-six hours of enormous doses of the most powerful of the sulfa drugs, the second eye went blind.

A Dramatic Cure

If penicillin had not been available the patient would have been doomed to death, but as the drug dripped continuously into his veins the shadow which had hung over him began to recede. After only four hours his blood, which had teemed with organisms, was practi-

Tests to determine purity and activity of penicillin were conducted at Merck, Inc., New Jersey.

cally germ-free. Within a day the temperature had dropped to 100° F. and appetite was returning. In three days the sight returned to one eye. On the sixth day the patient was able to open and move the other eye, although it was still blind. From this point on recovery went so smoothly that the attending doctor might almost have become bored if he had not known that he was witnessing something akin to a miracle.

Penicillin cases are like that. The drug is given, and convalescence proceeds as smoothly as a stone slips across the surface of a frozen pond. A woman who had had a breast removed suddenly shot a temperature of 106° F. as virulent germs invaded the wound. After penicillin was given, the doctor in charge observed that convalescence was "uneventful." An elderly man suffering from empyema, pus compressing his lung, received penicillin injections directly into his chest. In four days his appetite was greater than the hospital menu could satisfy.

Because penicillin is not irritating to the tissues, it can sometimes be applied or injected directly into the diseased part. A patient with meningitis, for instance, who was believed to be dying, had the drug injected into his nervous system by way of the spine. His recovery was briefly described as "uninterrupted." Of nineteen cases of chronic infection of the eye, only one failed to respond to penicillin drops or ointment. Infected fingers, draining wounds, carbuncles, and skin infections have all responded to the magic touch of the newest wonder drug. Of course there are some cases that respond more slowly and a few in which damage has gone too far for any remedy to save the victim, but, by and large, penicillin for power, for rapid action, stands head and shoulders above its nearest rivals the sulfa drugs.

But, great as the scope of penicillin is, and fresh discoveries keep expanding its usefulness, it is not a panacea. In the germ world, as in the human world, what is one man's meat is another man's poison. Although speedily fatal to so many disease germs, there are still some, such as the bacterium that causes tuberculosis, that can withstand its onslaught. Nor is penicillin going to put the sulfa drugs out of business overnight, for there is not yet enough to go around. Though it is being turned out by Merck, E. R. Squibb and Sons, Charles Pfizer and Company, and the Lederle Laboratories, many difficulties of production have still to be ironed out. The experts are skeptical as to whether there will be any for civilian use at all for many months, perhaps not even till the war is over. There is only one way in which the drug may be brought to the public sooner —the remote possibility that an inspirational brain storm may lead the chemists to its synthesis. It is a million-to-one chance. But then, where penicillin is concerned anything may happen.

President Harry Truman and Sir Alexander Fleming, discoverer of the miracle drug penicillin.

Miracles of Microfilm

by Lowell Brentano

Microfilm still had a long way to go in 1944, when this article appeared. But it already had an impressive list of achievements to its credit.

During the siege of Paris by the Prussians in 1870, a French photographer named Dagron printed messages on large sheets and photographically reduced them in size until a film containing 3,500 letters could be conveyed by a carrier pigeon. In 1925 a banking executive devised a high-speed mass-production method for photographing checks. Sponsored by the Recordak Corporation, a subsidiary of Eastman Kodak, his invention has consistently enlarged the sphere of its usefulness. In 1939 there was a mild hullabaloo when 30,000 pages, representing a cross section of our civilization, were microfilmed and buried with the Westinghouse Time Capsule at the New York City World's Fair, to be dug up 5,000 years hence. But it was not until Pearl Harbor that the science of microfilming, conceived in another war and another world, abruptly attained maturity and achieved recognition as a vital tool for victory.

Microfilming is the compressed recording of essential documents on strips of permanent nonexplosive film. Pictures are taken on 16-mm. or 35-mm. rolls, similar to those used in typical candid cameras, and every page photographed is reduced to the size of a postage stamp or less. The microfilm exposures are on 100-foot strips, wound on a spool, which can be filed in a specially designed cabinet. Afterwards, for consultation purposes, the spools are run through reading machines which enlarge the microfilms to full size or larger. Or, if desired, facsimile reproductions of the original document can always be made from the microfilm negative.

The excitement started when Chamberlain and his famous umbrella returned from Munich. Most intelligent Englishmen knew then that war was inevitable. The only question was, how much time was left?

Suddenly they realized that even military

Time capsule containing microfilm records is consigned to its 5000-year resting place.

preparedness can be undone if basic records are destroyed. Businesses supplying the war effort could not attempt to reopen their doors, once their fundamental papers were gone. Bombed factories could be rebuilt. Burnt inventories could be replaced. But the loss through fire, flood, or sabotage of master blueprints for planes and battleships, of secret maps of confidential data accumulated by years of research, was irretrievable.

Almost overnight, practically every business and factory, from the conservative old Bank of England to the newest machine shop, gave orders to have its paper framework microfilmed. As fast as the rolls were developed, they were secreted in safe hiding places miles out of bombing range—and in some instances sent out of the country. The directors heaved sighs of relief. They knew that even if the physical assets of a company were entirely obliterated, they could speedily reconstruct the business from the microfilm duplicates.

The Rush To Film

During the earliest days of the war, with Mussolini's navy holding the Mediterranean, English troops to the Near East had to be sent around Africa. Often three months elapsed between the time a transport left England and the time families heard whether their boys had reached the destination safely. To boost the morale of both troops and soldiers, Pan American Airways and British Overseas Airways offered their services to His Majesty's government. Using an adaptation of the Recordak process, they created and developed airgraphs, which were the precursors of our V-mail. The airgraph system was expanded until it now knits the British Empire together with more than a million letters a week!

Every American knows the story of V-mail, but it was not until ordinary men and women throughout the country had personally sent their sons, brothers, and husbands V-mail notes or, better still, pictures of "the new baby," that they began to appreciate the possibilities of the microfilming method in space saving, weight, and consequently speed. When they learned that 85,000 letters could be compressed to a weight of twenty pounds, it was easier to visualize other applications of the process.

Following Pearl Harbor, when America first regarded sabotage and enemy destruction as contingencies to be reckoned with, San Diego, California's leading boom town, rushed to film its property assessment rolls before the Japs could arrive for a token bombing! Business executives who had never given a thought to microfilming suddenly had nightmares at the thought of destroyed records. They discovered that 100 feet of unperforated 16-mm. film can contain pictures of more than 3,000 standard-sized 8 1/4 x 11 letters; that the same amount of 35-mm. can contain pictures of 600 engineering drawings, 24 x 36 inches each, or 825 full-size newspaper pages—and that these film reels can be stored in only a few cubic inches of space. In other words, microfilms occupy only 1 per cent of the space and are approximately 1/150 of the weight of the documents they supplant.

The fact that human activities are so closely linked with paper has tempted many concerns into the microfilm field—Remington Rand, Graflex, the Microfilm Corporation, University Microfilms, Precision Microfilming, and the Microstat Corporation, to mention only a few. Despite competition, the demands since Pearl Harbor and the restrictions on the Manufacture of new equipment have swamped all existing facilities. The companies say, "we don't need shoe leather to get business—it crowds in over the transom."

Different companies offer varied types of service. Graflex, for instance, sold a complete portable microfilm apparatus which could be transported in a large suitcase, but no more of these sets are to be had. Recordak leases and services its equipment, but the demand has so exceeded the supply that it has set up fifteen "service stations" in leading cities to which customers can send work. The Microstat Corporation also has licensees and branch offices throughout the United States which serve more than 700 prime contractors by taking the cameras right into their plants and directly providing them with precision Microfilm-by-Microstat. Not only do they send their own equipment and trained crews to the customers' files, but they insure the original negatives. By and large, customers must deal today either through "service stations" or through

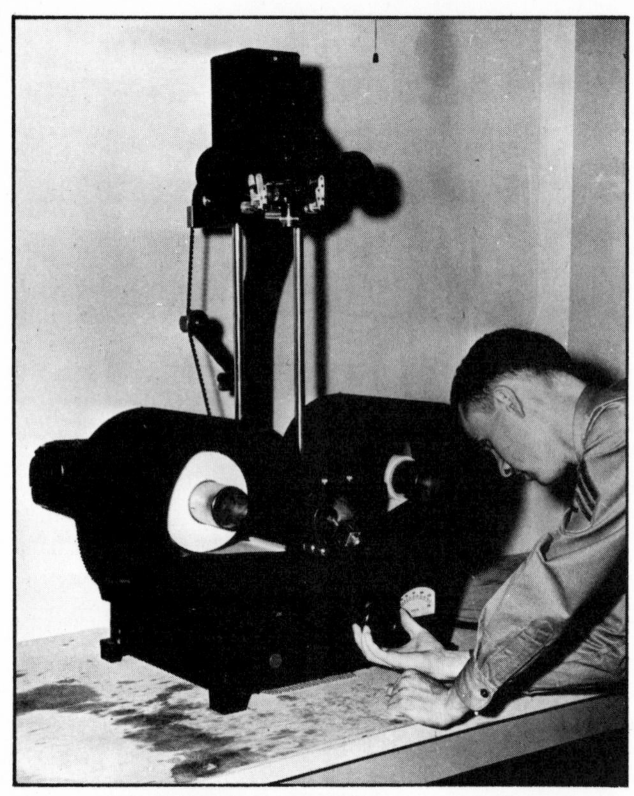

During World War II, V-mail was microfilmed.

companies like Microstat, since equipment for private installations is practically nonexistent.

First Films of Draft

Recordak's first big war job was to make a permanent and unassailable record of the draft. No one had ever heard of photographing a lottery before, but the authorities were determined to obviate the errors of 1917, when the draft numbers were read out and taken down by clerks with pen and ink. So in October, 1940, when the capsules were drawn out of the huge glass bowl, the numbers were placed on small cards showing the date and whether the hour was A. M. or P. M. On the card was a mechanical counter and a railroad watch. The whole set-up was photographed consecutively for the entire 9,000 numbers drawn. The records which then went out to the local draft boards were based directly on these microfilm negatives.

The government quickly foresaw the enormous advantage of space-and-weight-saving microfilm for the war effort. In 1942, for instance, the War Department had 180,000,000 inactive records stored in 12,000 standard sized four-drawer files. By microfilm reproduction, these records can be compressed into fifty files. Visualize such an elimination of filing cabinets on a nation-wide scale. Imagine the economies in steel or substitute materials used in their construction and in the man-hours necessary for their production. There's shortage of pulp, too, with consequent limitations on paper. Hundreds of tons of old records, no longer needed, are released and sent back to the mills—to be made into fresh paper. Many states have laws authorizing the destruction of original records after they have been photographed.

Front and Home Front

Even more important is the problem of floor space. Today the nation cannot afford to build new buildings to store old papers. Westinghouse faced this situation. It owned more than 2,000,000 essential sketches, charts, and blueprints, dating back fifty-six years, ranging from five-inch cards to five-foot drawings. And with its capacity war business, new data accumulating required more than 50,000 square feet of storage space per year. These papers are now being microfilmed at an average rate of thirty-

Microfilming of V-mail saved the U.S. millions.

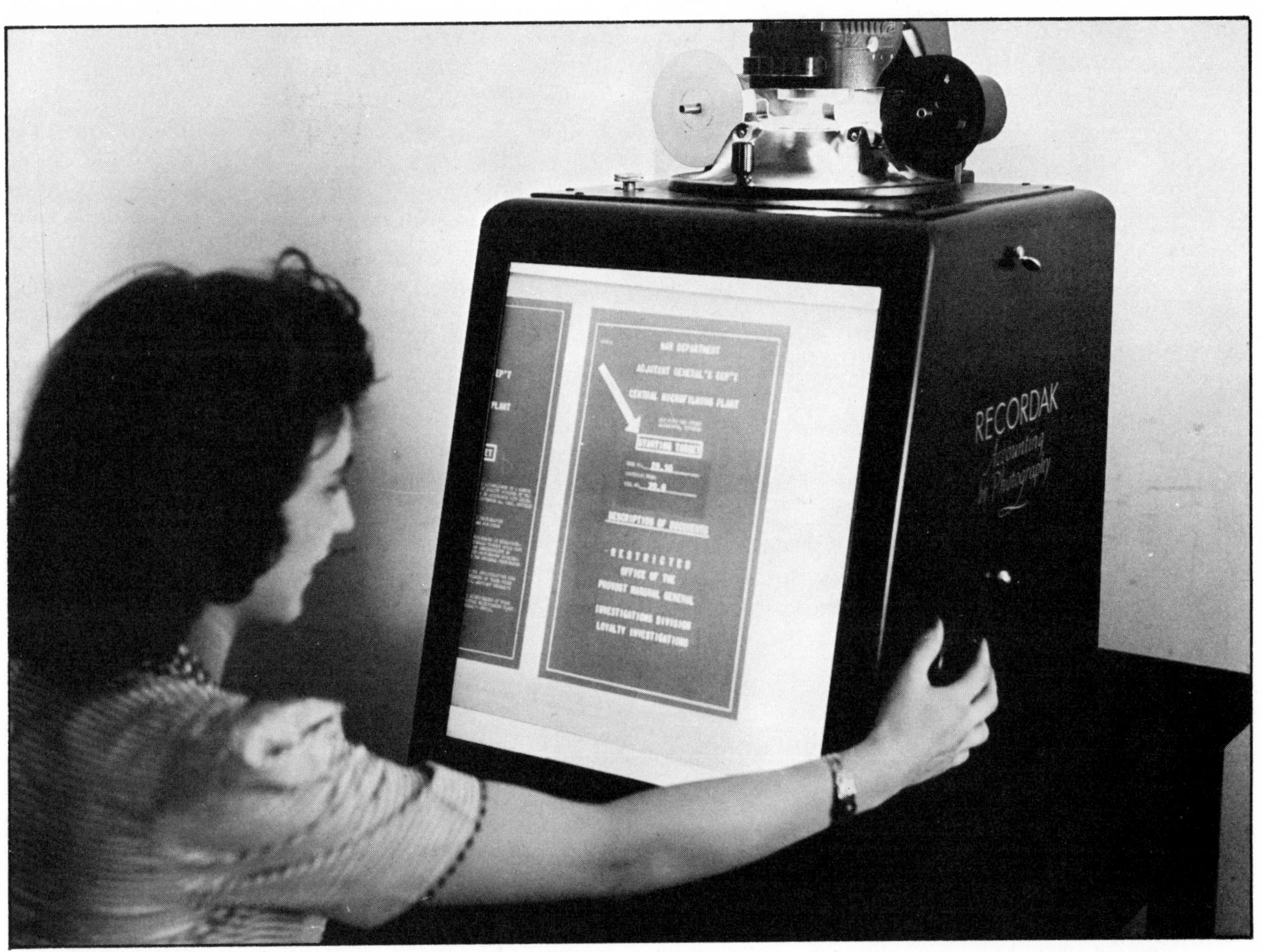

Most government records, those of the F.B.I., Treasury Department, etc., are consigned to microfilm.

five records per minute. The entire project will take two years, but when it is completed, the story of the electrical industry's growth will be housed in a vault about ten feet square. More than one acre of floor space will be cleared for productive purposes.

Microfilming also aids overburdened wartime transportation. Engineering records are bulky. They must be shipped long distances in large crates and boxes. A set of blueprints for a destroyer covers a quarter of an acre; the plans for a battleship weigh more than a ton. Yet quick reference to specifications on the spot is essential to a proper repair job. After the desolation of Pearl Harbor, the Navy could not afford to wait endlessly for blueprints. Little rolls of microfilm were flown halfway round the world in hours—and cut priceless weeks from the time required to put damaged ships back in service. Now the Navy intends to leave its blueprints on land and to microfilm the plans of every vessel. If a ship needs emergency repairs in some strange port, complete plans and a microfilm reader are on board, ready for immediate use.

Cities, states, and the federal government are using literally miles of film, not only for military purposes but to maintain the machinery of the home front. Thousands of the nation's banks photograph the statements of their ration-coupon transactions with dealers and wholesalers. The census tables, bound in bulky twenty-five-pound volumes ordinarily carried on small hand trucks, are in process of being transferred to film. The F. B. I. has microfilmed its entire fingerprint file and is prepared to send out fascimiles much more easily and quickly than in the past. The United States treasury has welcomed photography as an aid in keeping track of Treasury checks. To safeguard against the possibility of loss, theft, or the misplacement of forms, the Social Security Bureau has installed photographic equipment and intends to record its tremendous volume of reports. Both our Social Security records and our war-bond purchases are microfilmed by Recordak.

Safeguarding Culture

Microfilm is safeguarding our culture, preserving books, music, and paintings for posterity. A microfilm book is merely the result of photographing consecutively each page of an ordinary printed book. Afterward, reading machines enlarge these micro-copies to full size or larger. This canned literature is of the utmost importance. Recently the Chinese government sent 3,000 of its rarest volumes for safekeeping to the Library of Congress, and for the duration Chinese scholars will have to content themselves with studying the micro-copies on reading machines. In the summer of 1942 Columbia University photographed its card catalogue, the key to its priceless library. That catalogue could not be stored for it had to be kept in daily service. Now the Rockefeller Foundation has appropriated $170,000 for a project to photograph the contents of the British Museum, the indexes of the London Public Records Office, and the libraries of Oxford and Cambridge—in a word, our complete Anglo-Saxon cultural heritage.

Music and painting are similarly indebted to this process. No musician wants to ship original scores overseas today. When Toscanini decided to play the war symphony of Shostakovich, the famous Russian composer microfilm recorded the entire orchestration on more than 2,000 prints, which were brought here by Clipper. Pictures are bulkier and even more hazardous to transport. So the renowned Phipps Art Collection, of more than 350,000 paintings, is being photographed on color film. Projects such as these go far beyond the question of safety. At a minimum of expense, twenty dollars for the usual size 320-page novel, they make available to libraries, universities, museums, and individual scholars the culture of the ages.

As the advantages of microphotography become more evident, new frontiers are explored. For instance, there is the perplexing question of the identification of Merchant Marine seamen. A sailor carries a variety of documents, including a birth certificate, citizenship and shipping papers, a lifeboat ticket and a passport. But if his boat is torpedoed and he is lucky enough to escape with his life, frequently his papers are lost. Sometimes a lifeboat or a raft lands upon some lonely stretch of beach, and the Coast Guard doesn't know what to do with the survivors. Especially if they are foreigners, there may be a legitimate doubt as to whether they are genuine victims of a disaster at sea or are planted Axis spies. Obviously there must be a rigid investigation. Despite the shortage of shipping personnel, it sometimes takes months before the government feels it safe to put these men back on ships. Now the War Shipping Board is testing out a process of photographing seamen's identification papers on a tiny strip of film, which is permanently sealed in a transparent locket, carried on a chain around the neck. Duplicate prints of the film are also distributed to the chief ports of the United Powers. By these means, even if a man loses his clothing, he can confirm his status immediately.

Uses For Maps

Maps are now almost as essential as bullets. Every time our armed forces prepare for a new offensive, microfilm duplicates available maps and photographs of the region by the thousands.

But more ingenious maps are being evolved for specific purposes, such as dredging or mine sweeping, one of the most perilous naval operations. The ordinary hydrographic charts are not detailed enough for this work. Depth has to be indicated in exact feet or fathoms for 400 to 500 locations to the square mile. So a large-scale map is prepared for the limited area to be dredged. Then it is microfilmed and the negative is placed on a slide, which is slipped in a frame over the lens of an ordinary flashlight. A magnifying glass is clipped over the frame. Both the officer on the bridge and the officer in charge of the deck are provided with this equipment, which enables them to synchronize their movements and direct their ship with infinite caution.

Costs and ease of operation favor the future development of microfilm. A commercial Recordak, capable of 6,000 check-size exposures an hour, installed and serviced leases for $30 monthly. A smaller machine, Recordak, Jr., fitted for average office work, can be had for $12.50 monthly. A 100-foot roll of film, including development, costs $3. Now that leased equipment is available only on priority, the Recordak Corporation photographs customers' letters at $5 per 1,000 exposures complete with a minimum charge of $10. Microstat Corporation, however, estimates its fees on the number of exposures, and the price covers all charges, including the first year's insurance premium on the cost of the negatives. Ten thousand exposures on a customer's premises, with eight letters on a frame, are 16 cents an exposure or 2 cents a letter; 100,000 exposures, 9 cents a frame or about 1 cent a letter. These prices may vary in different sections of the country.

In the postwar era, microfilming will play an important role. Already thousands of feet of film have been sent to Britain, Norway, and the Low Countries to make photographs of property records and even of the property itself. These will be invaluable evidence for claimants in reparation settlements.

Indeed, the entire world is becoming microfilm-minded. Observers predict that business men will have film readers on their desks, where sales or credit information and confidential reports will be received on film in tamperproof form. In the shape of things to come, it is not improbable that a man will carry his library in a cigarette case and his business records where they belong—in the aspirin box.

Secretary Of State Stimson draws the first draft number. Draft records were kept on microfilm.

STOP
ONE WAY

Tomorrow's Cars and Roads

by Robert Moses

Few men in our day have made more thorough studies of traffic and roads than has the outspoken Robert Moses. Here is what he had to say in 1943.

The automobile industry faces postwar research problems which will tax to the limit our vaunted Yankee genius. These problems go way beyond the shape, size, weight, speed, and price of postwar cars. There are more things to be studied than my friend Mr. Kaiser's 500-pound, five-passenger, 100-miles-an-hour-on-one-gallon-of gas plastic car, purchasable at every good filling station at five hundred bucks.

A distinguished architect recently made this comment about housing to an association of builders:

"Our industry is giving the general public a picture of radical change and unusual improvment to come after the war, and this is going to be a boomerang. For a time at least there are going to be few changes of any importance and radical or mass changes in construction are going to come gradually and over a long period of time."

Precisely the same remark applies to the postwar automobile. There are plenty of things we must do to pave the way for the new car. For one thing, the makers of cars and fuel and the builders of roads must meet and cooperate. There is no sense in building trucks too big and heavy for the roads and roads too flimsy for the trucks, and in loading trucks and buses with heavy freight and passengers better carried on rails. What does a manufacturer gain by boasting of high-speed cars if the destruction they will cause is so great that the public will turn against them? Why multiply trailers, if communities get fed up with road gypsies? Why should the manufacturer's interest stop at the salesroom and the highway engineer's concern begin there?

The first chore is one for geologists as well as chemists, engineers, and salesmen. Where shall we get gasoline? How fast are our oil supplies disappearing? What are the substitutes? Coal, of course, is one of them, but mining is becoming more expensive. Another puzzle involves the future of iron ore and the substitutes for it. Still another is the problem of rubber. Fortunately, synthetic rubber is well on its way. The question arises—how much will be synthetic and how much natural and what will be the costs? Still another problem is that of plastics and the new metals such as aluminum and magnesium, whose weaknesses and potentialities are as yet only vaguely known.

Furthermore, we don't know when the war will end, what sort of government we will have afterward, what encouragement will be given to private business, how fast war orders will be canceled, how long the tapering-off process will go on, what plants, equipment, and tools now owned by federal agencies will be turned over to the present contracting manufacturers, abandoned, or otherwise operated. Nevertheless, the industry will have to make intelligent and conservative guesses in the midst of all these uncertainties.

Public officials, on the other hand, must think of the roads of tomorrow, of advanced highway design and of improved materials, methods, and equipment, without which the new passenger cars, trucks, and buses are worthless. We must have some idea of what production the industry has in mind in order to be able to schedule road construction and repair intelligently.

Not A Practical Guide

A great deal of nonsense has been sprouted recently about highway travel. For a while we had a spasm of enthusiasm for tremendous transcontinental highways. This died as the result of sheer logic, because there never were

(Above) experiment in robot traffic control, 1930. (Right) one of the first superhighways to move traffic quickly and efficiently through urban and suburban areas was the Merritt Parkway in New York.

figures to prove that there existed or would exist in the near future any really substantial amount of transcontinental travel as distinguished from regional and local travel, excepting, of course, a few main routes from coast to coast and from Canada to the Gulf, and the Inter-American highway system.

General Motors spent some $7,000,000 on the Futurama at the 1939-40 World's Fair. It was a swell show. Thousands of people stood in line for hours to get a free ride on an ingenious merry-go-round from which they could see spread before them sixteen-lane roads, photoelectric controls shifting cars from one speed level to another, and spiderlike bridges hanging by a single thread over great chasms and rivers.

The Futurama was a legitimate, first-rate, stimulating advertising stunt and was deservedly successful. But it wasn't meant to be a practical guide for present-day manufacturers and public officials who must be responsible to car owners and taxpayers for what they do. Actual construction must be planned, financed, and done under all sorts of limitations.

It is finally dawning upon both dreamers and rural-minded officials that most of our travel originates and ends in cities, and that when we by-pass the cities we simply duck around

(Top) Robert Moses speaks on the future of superhighways. (Bottom): Mayor La Guardia (center) and Bob Moses (right) break ground for East River Drive, New York.

the entire problem and thrust it upon crowded communities which cannot meet it without help. Standards for ordinary streets, country highways, and secondary roads are fairly well established. It is the congested urban and suburban main artery that requires our clearest thinking and best judgment.

People Want Roads

Out of all the welter of controversy about postwar public works one fact is emerging: The average citizen is enthusiastic about highway improvement. He knows that our highways are rapidly going to pieces because of war restrictions on construction and repairs. He has seen what some communities have done and wants their example followed elsewhere. He wants as good a system for his neck of the woods as the best elsewhere. Every American wants a durable cheap car, and he looks to the automobile industry to provide it. He has no desire to wear that car out quickly on a broken and obsolete road system. What is more, he is willing to pay the bill.

How shall our highway improvements be financed? Some will be paid for out of matched federal and state funds; some by bond issues, some out of license and gas taxes, some out of other current taxes, and some by assessment. Others will be wholly or partly self-liquidating by means of tolls and other service charges. For many years the American public paid tolls on turnpikes as well as bridges and ferries. But the backbone of our new national highway system cannot be made out of toll roads. It will be devised and financed on a joint, co-operative federal, state, and city basis.

We already have substantial federal-matched moneys for design of postwar highways and the more progressive states and municipalities are taking advantage of these inducements and supplementing them with funds of their own. The federal program will be sound and successful as long as federal highway officials continue to allow it to develop locally, do not interfere with local initiative, and demand only that the projects be feasible and the work well done. If there should be an attempt to run the entire national highway system from Washington, local initiative and support would disappear.

We would then have the same cumbersome overmanned bureaucratic federal machine in the domain of public works which we now have in so many other fields.

What sort of roads should we build? We should build parkways where they are appropriate; that is, where there are scenery and local values to preserve, where travel should be restricted to passenger vehicles. We should have through-ways free from traffic lights and crossings at grade, but open to all sorts of vehicles. Finally, there are ordinary roads and streets with frequent access which should be built the right width and with all tested improvements.

We have been experimenting with considerable success on major crossing eliminations. Several more or less standard types have emerged, and we have developed numerous examples of all these types. The problems are, of course, most difficult in metropolitan areas. Here the obstacles are most numerous, opposition is greatest, costs are highest, and the tendency is most pronounced to make compromises with principles. We know pretty well by now what modern traffic arteries will cost.

How much can we afford to spend on our new arteries? There is no use hiding the figures. An ordinary four-lane concrete highway runs to $100,000 a mile without counting the right of way. A typical rural section of four-lane parkway with only a few grade separation bridges costs $250,000 a mile; a typical suburban section of four-lane parkway, $400,000 a mile; a mixed urban traffic artery with six lanes, $800,000 a mile; a six-lane city parkway through expensive and often built-up areas, from $1,250,000 to $1,750,000 a mile; arterial improvements with six lanes and a

Former New York Governor Alfred Smith (l) and Robert Moses cut tape for opening of Wantagh Parkway.

service road along built-up-water front, involving reconstruction of plants and industrial and commercial structures, at least $2,000,000 a mile; elevated parkways with surface lanes below in cities average about $3,000,000 a mile.

Comparatively little is known about proper lighting and marking of parkways and throughways. We need more experimentation in this field. We must have more study of parking facilities, especially in cities, and of bus terminals, and we must decide whether private enterprise can provide the answers. Planting and landscaping is another subject which requires much more study than we have given it. Obviously, more elaborate and more expensive landscaping is justified on a parkway than on an ordinary express road, but express arteries can also be planted intelligently and economically. In some places attractive scenery already exists and merely needs to be preserved. In other cases it must be made.

The old-fashioned, society, bird-bath, landscape architect will never concede that the less exotic the stuff he orders, the better it will be. It has been found, for example, that many attractive trees and shrubs can be planted in sand without dragging in immense quantities of topsoil, and that native material can be made much more pleasing at smaller cost.

Then there is the question of the size of cars, trucks, and buses. It is obvious that buses and trucks can become so large and so heavy as to obscure other traffic, break down the roads, and convert them into semi-private rights of way in which in the end the big vehicles drive the others off entirely.

Another automobile menace is the railroad crossing at grade. There is a curious assumption, not substantiated by either the courts or common sense, that the elimination of such crossings is something separate and apart from modern highway construction. As a matter of fact and law, the automobile and not the train has caused the danger at such crossings, and the elimination of railroad crossings is therefore primarily a highway problem. These eliminations are more expensive than those where two or more highways meet, and their design, especially in settled communities, is much more than an engineering problem, because it will determine whether they will improve or blight the surroundings.

Until quite recently some obstacles were accepted as the road builder's headache. In this category always were hills, valleys, swamps, and small streams. Others, for no good reason were left to all sorts of public and even private enterprise to meet. For example, the highway engineer gracefully bowed out when his road hit a city line, a railroad, or a good-sized river. There is no generic distinction between a big bridge and a little one, and, toll or free, the bridge is an integral feature of the road system, and should be planned as such. Similarly, at water gaps too wide to be spanned by bridges, large, steady, fast auto ferries should be just as much the road engineer's concern as culverts, drainage, or curbs. North and south Michigan are tied together by the Mackinac Ferry, run by the State Highway Commission.

Speed Demons

It is to be hoped that the great objectives of the new cars and roads will be safe, uninterrupted travel at moderate speeds over durable roads. Here we require more restraint rather than more imagination and energy. The speed demons are fanatics. I refer not to careless, irresponsible, or drunken drivers, but to supposedly responsible people in one way or another engaged in the automotive and highway industry or in the driving of cars, who honestly believe that cars should not only be made to run faster on special occasions and for advertising purposes, but that speed regulations should be lifted entirely or greatly liberalized. They want all cars, trucks, and buses to run at from sixty to eighty miles an hour, even in congested areas. They favor parkways, boulevards, and through-ways without crossings, with infrequent entrances, and without traffic lights, not merely to facilitate smooth travel but to encourage rapid transit equaling train schedules.

The time actually saved by speedsters is very small. The difference between forty and sixty miles an hour on a twenty-mile stretch on one of our parkways is only ten minutes. Not only is the danger increased, but at high speed accidents are always serious and often fatal. High speed on ordinary roads without traffic dividers is foolish. On the highways of tomorrow it will be suicidal. One of our most famous brain surgeons told me that a large proportion of all the head injuries he treated before the war were caused by head-on automobile collisions. Our record of automobile accidents is frightful.

All this applies primarily to passengers. In a world in which speeding becomes a habit sanctioned by law and fixes a new tempo of travel, what will become of the luckless pedestrian and his children? Of 40,000 persons killed in car accidents in 1941, almost 11,000 were pedestrians.

Thirty miles an hour on the average boulevard is plenty in cities, forty is enough in the suburbs, and fifty should be tops anywhere in the country, no matter how open and thinly populated. My idea of futility is to build a beautiful parkway for speed demons who can't tell a flowering shrub from a bale of hay. I do not believe that any manufacturer should be allowed to advertise that he makes cars which will run eighty miles an hour. I speak as an official who for years has had to look at daily records of gruesome accidents, and as one who knows that no improvement in the making of cars and roads, no center curbs, no training, no regulations, and no police supervision can make high speed even comparatively safe. Fast driving should be stopped at the source—that is, in the factory.

These transportation problems require our very best thinking, and the quicker we get at them the better it will be for all concerned. If in the process we can screen out the type of planner and publicist who is merely educating himself at public expense, our progress will be much more rapid and we shall be much more certain that we are going in the right direction.

General Motors "Futurama" exposition at the 1939 World's Fair predicted the future of the automobile.

Radar–How It Works and What It Does

by Robert N. Farr

Radar was a regular part of the wartime picture, but in 1945, as the war was drawing to a close, Robert N. Farr gave some thought to its peacetime uses.

The fight for Iwo Jima was the toughest battle in the entire history of the U. S. Marines. Four thousand Americans gave their lives during the twenty-nine days it took to wrest the island from the Japs. Some 25,000 of the Mikado's best troops died almost to the last man.

What was the reason for such a struggle over the mere scrap of volcanic rock and dirt? Why did our Pacific commanders send ashore three whole divisions of marines, and back them up with guns and planes of a whole fleet of battleships and carriers?

One answer is—radar.

Iwo Jima was Japan's key outpost for the detection of American bomber fleets flying from Saipan and Tinian to Tokyo. Our B-29s were

A radar unit, like the one below, detected Japanese planes approaching Pearl Harbor.

spotted before they were halfway to their target, and warning of their approach was flashed back across 750 miles of water to the Japanese homeland by radio. Thus there were always tough reception committees lying in wait for them on their arrival over Fujiyama. The radar installations on Iwo Jima simply had to be destroyed.

Radar has been used in many ways during the war, both as a weapon of offense and of defense. At Guadalcanal, in North Africa, Sicily, Salerno, Nettuno, Anzio, Burma, the Marshalls, Kwajalein, Saipan, Guam—in all operations on the continent of Europe and in the Pacific—radar has helped to carry out Allied operational and logistical plans.

Radar was ready when the German Luftwaffe tried to blitz Britain in the summer of 1940. Without British radar to detect and point out high-flying German bombers, the Nazi air offensive might have succeeded.

How Radar Works

On December 7, 1941, the U. S. Army Signal Corps radar, with Private Joseph L. Lockard manning the controls, detected planes approaching Hawaii and located them about thirty minutes before they reached Pearl Harbor. Lockard flashed the news to his superior officer, who, knowing that a number of American planes were due from the mainland, believed that the radar had spotted them, and therefore took no action. The planes, of course, were Japanese air squadrons flying on their mission of treachery.

But, even though its warning had gone unheeded, radar had done its duty, and so had Private Lockard, who was decorated with the Distinguished Service Medal and sent to the Officer Candidate School of the Signal Corps, from which he graduated as a lieutenant.

Less than a year later, radar enabled us to get in some of the first effective licks at Guadalcanal. When the sea battle for the Solomons was in its final stage, the invisible beam of American radar was sent out into the blackness of night by a ship of our fleet. It picked up and definitely located a Japanese battleship eight miles away. The guns of the U. S. battle wagon were elevated and aimed. Two thundering salvos, and the Jap ship was sunk, although no American eye had ever seen it.

Japanese radar unit ruined by U.S. bombers.

Radar is credited with playing a major role in clearing the short northern road to Japan through the Aleutians. American Army and Navy officers looked gloomily at the fog-cursed chain of islands with their sky-scratching mountains and uncharted shores which were a menace to our ships and planes. They realized the great military potentialities of these islands, but considered them almost useless because of the weather. Then someone suggested radar as the key to open the door to the Aleutians. It was tried, and it worked. Today our military installations in the Aleutians have great strategic value. For radar can see through snowstorm or fog, and warn seamen and pilots of danger ahead.

In spite of fog, darkness, bad weather, and smoke screens, radar has enabled taskforce and convoy commanders to maintain constant checks on the ships in their charge. It keeps them fully informed, too, of the presence of

Seagoing radar units that detected movements of the Japanese fleet helped win many naval battles.

enemy submarines which may have surfaced in the night.

If It Sinks, It's A Ship

On some of our Pacific Islands radar operators get a ringside seat at sky battles. When the slant-eyed protectors of Tokyo fly in to attack one of our island strongholds, radar invariably picks them up in time to send U. S. planes aloft to meet them. Radar operators follow the fight on screens that are not unlike those in a television receiver. They can see every action that takes place in the heat of battle. They can even see bombs explode. They can follow the movements of enemy planes from the time they pick them up, can watch Nip fighters drop earthward like falling rocks.

Radar is helping B-24 "Snoopers" in the Southwest Pacific raid Jap shipping and airfields. Airborne radar, similar to the so-called "Mickey" being used by bombers in Europe, enables planes to navigate unerringly across a thousand miles of open sea and weather, then to spot a blacked-out invisible airfield with the accuracy of a well trained pointer dog. Radar-equipped planes of the Fifth and Thirteenth Air Forces have pounced upon their Jap prey from New Ireland to the Netherlands East Indies, from Palau to the Philippines. They have bedeviled Truk, tormented Woleai, and wallopped Borneo.

Snoopers out on their own at night can spot a large Nip transport, cruiser, or battleship from a distance of thirty or more miles, and can close in for the kill without assistance. Radar sees better in the dark than human eyes have ever seen in the daytime. And it enables the Snoopers to come in undetected by the enemy and strike from an altitude of 1,500 feet or less, an altitude that makes the crews who do visual daylight bombing shudder.

In August, 1943, the first squadron of Snoopers arrived in the Pacific and joined the Thirteenth Bomber Command. Those were the days when the Japs thought they could hold the Solomons for a long time. While our bombing prevented them from operating during the day, their surface vessels shifted men and supplies from one island to another under cover of darkness, undetected.

On the night of August 23, 1943, two Jap destroyers moved into the slot of water that runs all the way up the Solomons between Santa Isabel and New Georgia. The Japs were planning to evacuate troops from Kolombangara and Vella Lavella. Supremely confident that nothing could stop them, the destroyers paid little heed to the drone of a single airplane in the dark skies above them.

Then they got a terrific shock.

Bombs, released when radar gave the "go ahead," tumbled from the skies as if dropped down invisible chutes connecting the unseen plane with the destroyers. They hit squarely on the decks. The night was torn apart by flaming explosions. Two bomb runs were made; each time our plane scored direct hits. Then, its mission concluded successfully, the plane returned.

The Japs probably thought we were just lucky, for they continued sending ships by the same route. On the night of September 29, 1943, Snoopers destroyed most of a convoy of eleven Jap ships in almost the same spot.

Radar, which has enabled us to accomplish so many of these military miracles, is the code name for "radio detecting and ranging." The letters r-a-d-a-r spell the same word when read either forward or backward. And, coincidentally, this gives a clue to what radar is: a radio echo. It is an electronic instrument which projects a beam of radio impulses through space at the rate of 186,000 miles a second. In much the same way as the beam of an automobile's headlights discloses a road sign, these impulses reveal the presence of distant objects by rebounding from them to the observer. A cathode-ray tube acts as interpreter and makes the electronic echoes visible to the human eye.

In the Battle Of The Bulge, the 101st Airborne Division set up radar unit near Bastogne, Belgium.

When trained on enemy planes still so distant as to be beyond the reach of anti-aircraft or the radar-equipped Black Widow, P-61 night fighters, radar reports the three elements of their position that are necessary for exact plotting: (1) distance, (2) elevation, (3) deflection, *i.e.*, position to right or left.

If you have ever shouted toward a cliff and timed the echo's return to determine how far you were from the cliff, you have used a method similar to radar. However, radar uses ultra-high-frequency radio waves, only a few centimeters long, while your echo was made up of sound waves.

Electronic radar equipment sends out its wave with the speed of light. The wave goes forward in a straight line until it hits something such as an enemy plane, a rock, or a ship. Then, much as light is sent back to its starting place by a mirror, the radio wave is reflected by the object it strikes and is bounced back. The time it takes for the radio wave to start its journey and to return gives the distance of the object. If radar could be beamed on the moon, the waves would complete the round trip in two and a half seconds.

It would be of little value to know merely that an enemy plane was one mile or five miles or 100 miles away. We must also know its direction and its height. When we know all that, we can aim our guns and destroy it.

Since the days of Egyptian surveyors we have known how to calculate and determine the direction and the height of things by fixing the angle. In radar, the direction is established through the use of directional wave transmission. The height is established by applying radio direction finding and other radio principles. Thus the exact position of the enemy is plotted very accurately. Today this plotting is done automatically with the aid of a computer that performs the operation with split second speed. The time required for a radar wave to travel to an object fifty feet away is one ten-millionth of a second, yet the computer can measure it.

G.I.s of Battery C, 68th Coast Artillery, operate radar in a field in Italian theatre of operation.

The complete radar unit, which can be built small enough to fit into the palm of your hand, is a combination transmitter and receiver which rotate in unison, scanning the same area at the same time. The transmitter emits ultra-high-frequency radio waves over a broad arc in the general direction it is desired to explore. When this radiation strikes an object having appreciable conductivity, some of the energy is reflected or scattered back toward the receiver. From the receiver it is fed into a computer and to the six-inch screen of a cathode-ray tube. This tube is the guide which gunners and bombardiers use to spot their targets.

Any object, or group of objects, will show on the screen of the cathode tube, each as a separate speck of light moving in relation to the movement of the ship at sea or the plane in the air, and in relation to the movement of the ship or plane on which the radar is located. Water shows up on the screen as dull blue-white; land shows up as black. This gives the viewer the information he would get from a simple outline map. Buildings, airplanes, and other objects show up on the screen in their recognizable shapes.

During a demonstration of radar, someone asked, "If you are flying over a ship and a rock of the same relative size and shape, both will show up on the radar screen. How can you tell which is ship and which is rock?"

The demonstrator replied, "We bomb it anyhow. If it sinks, we know it was a ship."

In radar equipment the most important tube, next to the cathode-ray tube, is the directional klystron tube, perfected for the government by Westinghouse engineers from an invention of Russell H. and Sigurd F. Varian, two brothers at Leland Stanford University.

This tube and others like it project waves like a searchlight beam.

Electrons race from a device at one end of the tube in a continuous stream with a speed of about 20,000 miles a second under the impetus of from 1,000 to 8,000 volts. They are influenced by an electric field which bunches them together and creates the beam, which, like light, pursues a line-of-sight course.

Unlike radio waves, klystron waves do not spread out and pass through nonmetallic materials. If you were to take a lamp that can be lit by klystron waves and place a slab of wood between the lamp and the klystron antennae, the energy would be cut off from the lamp and it would go out. Another important feature is the fact that klystron waves actually appear to stand still, so they can be physically measured. This makes it possible to count the waves in the radar computer.

Fast Obsolescence

Radar equipment is specialized and comes in various types and sizes. There are three basic types of radar: surface radar for use by ground defenses to provide data for antiaircraft guns in smashing Axis planes; airborne radar, for use, for example, in bombing through clouds from a B-29 Superfortress or in attacking enemy planes in a Black Widow night fighter; and fire-control radar such as the Navy uses to spot enemy ships. Development of radar science is extremely rapid: much radar equipment that was in use six months ago is obsolete today.

Radar is not perfect in any of its forms, but research, in which every major electronics laboratory in the United States is co-operating with the government, sees the day of practical perfection in sight. One of the problems that must be overcome is the fact that radar cannot see beyond the horizon, over the curve of the earth.

Radar reaches its highest degree of usefulness in aerial warfare. Connected to the automatic pilots of planes, radar makes it possible to fly the planes to invisible targets. Joined to the latest computing bombsights, radar enables bombardiers to release their tons of death and destruction at the precise moment to secure results that are almost as good as can be obtained under conditions of full visibility. The first use of radar by the Americans for bombing an invisible target was in October, 1943, in the U. S. Army Air Force raids on Germany and Austria.

Radar even shows the pilots the way home from bombing missions, enabling them to fly blind and to land with perfect safety at their home bases at night or when the ground is obscured by clouds and overcast. In fact, the first use of radar in aircraft was for a blind landing at Boston in the prewar year 1939.

The Pathfinder bombing technique, originally developed by the Royal Air Force, was first used for night bombing on August 18, 1942. Since then it has helped put the Nazi war machine out of commission by deadly accurate bombing through the clouds. The equipment that makes this bombing possible consists of the radar Pathfinder device and colored smoke signals which are used to locate and mark the target. This radar can see through clouds and overcast from altitudes as high as 30,000 feet, and when the bombardier sees his target in the cathode screen he shouts, "Here's our target! Let's drop our bombs!"

Only one plane of a formation usually a B-17 Flying Fortress or a C-47 Skytrain, carries the Pathfinder radar. When the target is spotted

Radar detector truck of the 578th Aircraft Warning Battalion, Yasawa Island, tracks the Japanese Air Force.

the Pathfinder plane drops colored smoke bombs if a daytime operation, or colored smoke flares if at night. These bombs or flares leave a ring of colored smoke in the clouds, through which the other planes in the formation release their bombs.

The sky-marker smoke bomb used by the A. A. F. was developed by Lieutenant Colonel C. H. Breedlove of the Chemical Warfare Service. It is a special flare held up by a small parachute so that it descends slowly, leaving a large cloud of colored smoke.

Used At Normandy

The Pathfinder technique was also used in the landing of paratroops at Normandy. Radar planes flew ahead of the troop-carrier aircraft and selected a suitable spot beyond the range of enemy fire for the paratroopers to drop.

The U.S. had radar units on every "rock" in the South Pacific. Shown here is the installation at Ryukyus.

They marked the spot with colored smoke flares.

Does the enemy know about radar? Yes. The fundamental principle of radar is no secret. In fact, the main objective of one of the first Commando raids along the coast of France, on February 27, 1942, was to capture intact the equipment of a German radar station north of Le Havre. The mission was successful.

One of the largest radar factories in the Reich was bombed by British Lancasters on June 21, 1942. Located at Friedrichshafen, on the north shore of Lake Constance at the Swiss border, the factory occupied the buildings formerly used by Germany for constructing Zeppelins. Other enemy radar factories have suffered a similar fate.

Radar has been used by the enemy in attacks on the Allies. The first warship sunk by radar-directed gunfire was *H. M. S. Hood*, detected by the *Bismarck* in May, 1941, and destroyed by the German battleship's first salvo. The commanding officer of the *Hood* spotted the *Bismarck* with his radar before the Nazi battle wagon opened fire, but he held his fire, fearing that he might be blindly hitting an Allied ship that was known to be cruising in the area.

In December, 1943, the Nazi warship *Scharnhorst* was attacked and sunk through the use of radar. Such uses of radar helped in large part to clear the Atlantic of Axis threats to Allied shipping.

For the past twenty months there has been a blackout on information concerning radar. One reason is the fact that British and American officials are waging a quiet fight over who shall control the patent rights to radar after the war. The British say radar is their baby, on the basis of British research and development, while our officials have pointed out that, by the admission of British scientists, radar development in England did not commence until the publication of reports by American experts.

Transportation Use

At any rate, radar promises to become a billion-dollar industry after the war. Radar sets similar to military equipment might be installed on automobiles. When the beams struck rows of roadside reflectors, the driver would be warned of danger spots and could be guided along the road despite rain or the densest fog. Radar might also be adapted so that stop-and-go lights on street corners would show up as red and green lights on the instrument panels of cars.

In the future one train will no longer crash into the back of another on the same track, or fall into a river when a bridge is washed out. Every locomotive engine will probably be equipped with a radar screen that will show the engineer at a glance the condition of the track miles ahead of him. Ships need no longer have difficulty finding their way in and out of harbors or through treacherous straits in fog and rain. Radar will give the commanding officer vision beyond the limits of his eyes. It will locate iceberge, shore lines, and other ships. And a radar device for ships will not be limited to seagoing craft. It will cost only a few hundred dollars, well within the reach of river boats and craft operating on the Great Lakes.

CAA Interested

The Civil Aeronautics Administration has already taken the first steps in applying radar to civil aviation. At the CAA experiment station at Indianapolis a series of experiments has been started which will use radar to increase safety in flying in fog, rain, or snow when pilots cannot see the ground and must rely upon instruments. Airport control towers equipped with radar screens could direct the movement of all planes up to 100 miles away on instrument approach. Radar could immediately detect any condition that might endanger planes taking off from or landing at fogbound airports. Radar warning devices mounted aboard planes could tell the pilot how far he was from other aircraft or from mountains, radio and water towers, etc. Radar altimeters could tell him exactly how far his plane was above the ground at all times.

Radar will emerge from this war almost human in its capabilities. When the great finger-like radar beams are finally turned to peace, they will point the way down new pathways of science to a more secure and comfortable world.

This plotting board, serviced by radar, served as an aircraft warning center during World War II.

Goldwyn's Golden Touch

by Edward Hutchings, Jr.

By 1944, the time of the following article, Samuel Goldwyn had produced some of Hollywood's greatest films. Here is the story of this battling producer.

Sam Goldwyn is a greatly understood fellow. There isn't a man in Hollywood who doesn't think he knows what makes Sam run. But there aren't two men who agree on what it is.

Take the theory that Goldwyn actually is a great artist who hasn't the slightest concern for money; then match it with the one about how he'd sell out his best friend to make a dollar. Listen to the stories of how he guards his good name like a jewel; then of how he'd walk barefoot down Hollywood Boulevard to get his name in print. Believe that he's a brilliant conversationalist—or that he can't get through a two-word sentence without stumbling. Accept the report that he is an expert on international affairs, and then reconcile it with the one that he never knows what's going on in the world outside his next picture.

There are two things about Sam Goldwyn on which even his worst enemies are in agreement, though—that he is one of Hollywood's shrewdest business men and one of its smartest producers.

Goldwyn has been making pictures for thirty-one years, and he's turned out such memorable productions as *Stella Dallas, Street Scene, Arrowsmith, Dodsworth, Dead End, Wuthering Heights,* and *The Little Foxes.* But, at the moment, Sam would far rather be known as the producer of *Up in Arms* (his current picture), *Treasure Chest* (his next picture), and *The North Star* (his last picture). In that order, please.

Goldwyn has the distinction of being one of Hollywood's most colorful legends while he is still around to enjoy—or endure—that reputation. And the legend is, of course, that Sam is responsible for most—if not all—of Hollywood's favorite jokes.

It was supposed to be Sam who once said, "For this part we need a *lady*—somebody that's *couth!*"

It was Sam who picked up a dictionary one day and started the following conversation: "What a big book! Who wrote it?"

"Webster."

"Must have taken him a long time."

"A century."

"My, my—fifty years."

It was Sam who was walking through a friend's garden when he spotted a sundial and asked what it was. "It tells time by the sun," said the friend. Sam shook his head. "What won't they think of next?" he said.

It was Sam who once asked a sculptor to make a bust of his wife's hands.

No "Include Me Out"

But was it? There *was* a time when Sam belonged to the "I-don't-care-what-they-say-about-me-as-long-as-they-spell-my-name-right" school of publicity. He even encouraged his own press agents to pin garbled-English anecdotes on him. Today, however, Sam denies most of the legend built up about him. He won't even take credit for that great contribution to the English language, "Include me out!" As Sam remembers it, he never said anything of the kind. He said, "I wish to tender my resignation."

Speaking in a voice that still has more than a trace of accent, but getting all the right words in the right places, he denies it by the hour. And he can make you believe him, too—because Sam Goldwyn is one of the great salesmen of all time.

As a matter of fact, Sam started in the motion-picture industry as a salesman. Born Sam Goldfish in Warsaw, Poland, in 1884, his parents died when he was still a child. When he was fourteen Sam came to America, headed

AT ALL LEADING THEATRES
Jane
Cowl
Madge
Kennedy
Mary
Garde
APPEARING
Goldwyn

ROUGHOUT THE WORLD -
Maxine
Elliott
Mabel
Normand
Mae
Marsh
EXCLUSIVELY IN
Pictures

for Gloversville, New York, and a three-dollar-a-week job in the glove factories there. First as a cutter, then head of a department, and finally as a traveling salesman, he prospered. He managed to crowd in only one year of night school, but at twenty-seven he was a partner in his firm, making $15,000 a year.

One day in 1910, however, Sam stopped in at the Herald Square Theater in New York to see some of the new "moving pictures." The show was hardly over before he had made up his mind to quit the glove business. He didn't know anything about making movies, but he knew it wouldn't be hard to make better ones than the crude two-reel Westerns he'd seen. He hounded his brother-in-law Jesse Lasky, who was in the vaudeville business, until finally, in 1913, the two men each put up about $10,000 and formed the Jesse L. Lasky Feature Play Co.

The Lasky Co. hired an unsuccessful young playwright named Cecil B. De Mille as director and a rising young actor named Dustin Farnum as star, and started to make a film version of the popular stage play *The Squaw Man* in an old livery stable in Los Angeles.

One of the first feature-length films to be made in this country, *The Squaw Man* ate up the Lasky Co.'s $20,000 in no time. It might never have been completed if Sam, the super-salesman, hadn't taken to the road and collected enough money in advance from theater operators to keep going. *The Squaw Man* cost $47,000—a staggering sum for the time—but the five-reel picture was a spectacular success and the Lasky Co. was launched on a profitable career.

The Lasky Co's great rival was Adolph Zukor's Famous Players Co., and the competition between the two companies for stars and screen material was feverish and expensive until, in 1916, a merger was arranged.

Famous Players-Lasky was a $25,000,000 corporation with Zukor as president and Sam chairman of the board. Sam was to be the business man, Zukor and Lasky in charge of production. But all three men were accustomed to being boss. They began to scrap over the division of executive control immediately. Then Zukor delivered an ultimatum to the board of directors. Unless Sam got out, he would resign. So Sam's stock interest of almost $1,000,000 was bought up and he left the company just a few short months after he joined it.

Goldfish To Goldwyn

In the same year he was back in business again, as president and chief owner of Goldwyn Pictures Corp.—in association with the Broadway producers Arch and Edgar Selwyn. The name of this new corporation was evolved by combining the first syllable of Sam's last name and the last syllable of the Selwyn name. In 1919 Sam Goldfish had his name legally changed to Goldwyn.

Famous Players-Lasky had by this time built up a tremendous stable of stars. Goldwyn promptly followed suit, and not only signed up movie personalities like Mabel Normand and Mae Marsh, but went to the legitimate theater for Madge Kennedy and Maxine Elliott and to the Metropolitan Opera for Mary Garden and Geraldine Farrar. If their pictures were not always successful, at least the publicity these great ladies brought Goldwyn was well worth the expense.

Eventually exhausted by the "artistic temperament" of his stars and the bitter competition of Famous Players-Lasky, Goldwyn decided to shift his sights and concentrate on stories rather than on stars. In 1919 he astonished the industry by organizing a League of Eminent Authors—consisting of Rex Beach, Rupert Hughes, Gertrude Atherton, Mary Roberts Rinehart, Basil King, Gouverneur Morris, and LeRoy Scott—to write pictures for him.

The Eminent Authors brought Goldwyn another great burst of publicity—and about twice as much temperament. Will Rogers, working for Sam at the time, sighed with relief when he was signed up to do Washington Irving's *Legend of Sleepy Hollow* rather than one of the Eminent Authors' productions. "I am off all living authors' works," he drawled. "Me for the dead ones."

Goldwyn Pictures prospered until 1922, when Sam became involved in another battle for executive control. When the row reached a deadlock he retired to write his memoirs (*Behind the Screen*, a book of chatty gossip on picture

Goldwyn (second from left) became allied with United Artists in 1926. Pictured here with him are Robert Fairbanks, Mary Pickford, Charles Chaplin, and Alexander Korda.

personalities) and subsequently settled the dispute by selling his stock interest in Goldwyn Pictures to the Metro Co. The next year the firm was merged to form the present Metro-Goldwyn-Mayer Co. In ten years Sam had helped create two of the industry's greatest companies—Famous Players-Lasky, which later became Paramount Pictures, and M-G-M.

In 1923 Goldwyn made another fresh start—this time as an independent producer in Samuel Goldwyn, Inc., Ltd. Unfortunately, he did not stay completely independent for long. In 1926 he allied his organization with United Artists—which had been set up in 1919 to distribute the pictures of independent producers. In 1927 he was elected an owner-member of the company.

More Legal Battles

Inevitably Sam's battle for control of the organization started again. By 1936, when there were five owner-members left in United Artists—Mary Pickford, Doug Fairbanks, Charlie Chaplin, Alexander Korda, and Sam—their wrangling had reached such a pitch that they were all sending their lawyers to represent them at stockholders' meetings.

In 1937 Goldwyn and Korda, being the most active producers in the organization, tried to buy up the interests of the other three owner-members but were stalled by unsurmountable legal obstacles.

Still chafing under what he considered an unfair distribution of profits—since Mary Pickford and Fairbanks were inactive and Chaplin had made only one picture in five years—Goldwyn sued to break his contract with United Artists in 1939, claiming that both Korda and Doug Fairbanks had set up separate producing companies over his objections. While he waited for the suit to be settled, he quit pro-

For The North Star *Goldwyn spent $260,000 to build this village, and then burned it down.*

ducing pictures entirely for a year and a half. In February of 1941 the suit was finally withdrawn when United Artists released him from his distribution contract and bought up his stock. Goldwyn arranged to have future pictures released through RKO and went back into production with *The Little Foxes.*

One-Man Movie Industry

Since then Goldwyn's business career has been comparatively calm. Today he has no partners, no stockholders, and is sole owner of his studio. Of all the independent producers in Hollywood he is the most independent. He makes the pictures he wants to make when he wants to make them—which usually means three or four a year as against the fifty or more turned out by the big studios. He rarely makes more than one picture at a time, because he is so completely in charge of each production that it is physically impossible for him to handle more.

He is as close as you can come to a one-man movie industry. He personally selects his stories. He personally supervises the writing of the screen play. He personally supervises casting. He personally passes on sets and costumes. He personally works out the musical score with the composer. He personally follows the progress of production day by day. When the picture is completed he personally cuts it—which may mean reducing 250,000 feet of film to anywhere from 9,000 to 12,000 feet. And after the picture is cut he often personally takes to the road and launches the publicity. So far, he has not tried selling tickets at the box office.

The result of this complete supervision is something Hollywood has come to call the Goldwyn Touch—an elusive phrase that stands most of all for quality but also for honest acting, handsome "mounting," and a literate story.

Goldwyn is one of a small handful of men in the industry who stamp a definite personality on their pictures. Invariably Goldwyn productions are in good taste, adult, dignified, with unmistakable "class." They have everything the young Polish glove cutter could ever have wished for when he came to America at the turn of the century. Goldwyn pictures also make money.

Money No Object

With a fierce pride in his name and his product, Goldwyn will go to any lengths to maintain his standards of quality. When he made *Wuthering Heights* he not only selected an all-British cast but built an English manor house that would have put most of the manor houses in England to shame. Its most extravagant feature—and one that could not possibly have been important to the average movie customer—was 1,000 windowpanes of genuine hand-blown English glass.

Even when he saw *The North Star* running into $3,000,000 he kept spending money to get exactly the effects he wanted. He had studio workmen slave for weeks to build a Russian village that was authentic down to the last mud puddle. That job cost something like $260,000, and not long after it was finished even more time and money were spent burning it down for the climax of the picture.

Money is no object when Goldwyn gets excited about a picture. And Goldwyn gets excited about every picture he makes. He won't start a movie unless he's enthusiastic about the story. Ever since the days of the Eminent Authors he has been sold on the theory that the story is the most important ingredient in making a picture—and once you have a good one the background, the actors, and all other considerations become secondary.

He's proved that theory innumerable times. It was a Hollywood legend, for example, that there was no such thing as a successful baseball picture, but *The Pride of the Yankees* was the greatest financial success Goldwyn ever had. Every studio in town turned down *Wuthering Heights* because it was too morbid, but it became another of Goldwyn's great triumphs. Every one thought *The Little Foxes* had too many disagreeable characters in it to make a popular film. They said *Dodsworth* wouldn't have any appeal because it was about middle-aged people. *The Children's Hour* (*These Three* on the screen) had a theme that was too hot for Hollywood to handle. *Dead End* was too sordid. *Arrowsmith* was about a doctor—and therefore too dull. Even *Whoopee*, Eddie Cantor's first movie, looked like a bad bet when Goldwyn was making it because the public was so fed up with musicals at the time that theaters were advertising "This picture has no music" to get customers up to the box office. And though Russian pictures were ticklish box-office risks when Goldwyn started work on *The North Star* in 1942, he spent a year and a half making it, and didn't even bolster his investment with big box-office names.

Goldwyn tries to launch at least one new face in each of his pictures. His current film, *Up in Arms*, stars Danny Kaye—who may have had a healthy following in Manhattan but was still an unknown quantity everywhere else when Goldwyn signed him up. Though every one agreed Kaye was a sure bet, and though every studio in town would have been glad to sign him and let him work his way up through the B pictures—or give him a four-minute spot in a grab-bag musical—Goldwyn shot the works and built a whole picture around him as though he were an established

Danny Kaye is captured by the Japanese in the Sam Goldwyn production, Up In Arms.

Mary Pickford and Sam Goldwyn were once partners in United Artists Productions—Here with them is Jimmy Roosevelt (right).

favorite like Bob Hope.

Up in Arms also gives Dinah Shore her first sizable movie role, introduces a young woman named Constance Dowling, and a whole personally hand-picked chorus of Goldwyn Girls. Like everything else he does, Sam's system for picking chorines is strictly unorthodox—but effective. He sent out the first chorus call for *Up in Arms* when he was in New York last fall. Several hundred young ladies showed up at the Goldwyn suite in the Waldorf Towers, dressed to the teeth.

"All I'm looking for is fresh faces," Sam said bluntly. "Will you please wipe off your make-up so I can see you?"

"Would you mind removing your hat and earrings?" he asked some of the young ladies. And, "How tall are you with your hair down?" he asked those who had obviously spent the morning sweeping their hair up.

Goldwyn has a passion for simplicity. Young actresses who work for him are forever getting personal beauty hints from the boss on how to use make-up, do their hair, and dress simply.

In his personal life Sam practically makes a fetish of simplicity. His home in Beverly Hills is fairly simple by Hollywood standards even if it is outfitted with all the required fixtures of a movie executive's estate—swimming pool, tennis court, and a wall that swings out to form a motion-picture screen. He lives quietly, doesn't smoke or drink. Almost every evening after dinner he runs off a movie and—though he is Hollywood's greatest crusader against double bills—sometimes two.

He goes to bed early, and sleeps outdoors whenever he can. He is up by 7 A. M. and drinks hot milk and sugar for breakfast instead of coffee. One way or another, he manages to walk for at least an hour a day. It's his chief exercise (though he occasionally plays golf with Mrs. Goldwyn) and the way he does it *is* exercise. Other people have to run to keep up with him.

He is careful about his diet and eats sparingly. As a result he is still trim as a stripling. Ice-cream sodas are his one weakness, and he's the kind of man who likes to drink two at a sitting. After the premiere of one of his pictures, several years ago, he took his whole staff to a soda fountain to celebrate. He is fastidious and has his suits made, by one of Hollywood's expensive tailors, to fit like the paper on the wall. He never carries anything in his pockets—no handkerchief, watch, or wallet. He never wears jewelry.

He's never learned to drive a car, so his pretty young wife—the former Frances Howard, whom he married in 1925, some ten years after his divorce from Blanche Lasky—sometimes drives him to work. She usually stays at the studio all morning, reading scripts and otherwise helping out.

Goldwyn's private office at the studio looks like a typical Park Avenue living room. It is richly furnished and includes a grand piano and numerous cabinet photographs of Mrs. Goldwyn and Sam Jr., their seventeen-year-old son who has just left the University of Virginia to enlist in the Army.

Sam lunches almost every day with his staff in the executive dining room at the studio. He likes to have young men working for him, and most of his executives are men under forty. He is as shrewd about picking competent assistants as he is at developing stars. (Will Rogers, Gary Cooper, Merle Oberon, David Niven, and Teresa Wright, were some of Goldwyn's.) A lot of the industry's top directors, producers, publicity men, etc., have been on Goldwyn's staff—men like Hunt Stromberg, Arthur Hornblow, Kenneth Macgowan, Howard Dietz, Jock Lawrence.

(Top) Mr. and Mrs. Sam Goldwyn arrive in New York en route to Moscow. (Bottom) in Russia they ride in a two-horse open sleigh.

But Goldwyn is head man of the Goldwyn Studios—the last word, the court of final appeals, the boss. Inevitably he has built up a kind of superego, so that he occasionally even refers to himself in the third person—as "Goldwyn thinks it ought to be done this way." He is an exacting boss and a highly volatile one, as quick to make up his mind as he is to change it. The people who work with him usually come to respect him greatly;at the same time they keep a weather eye out to try to predict which way he's going to turn next. He is always most anxious to get every one's opinion on any vexing problem, though he usually knows the answer he wants. He doeen't insist on yes men around him; sometimes the answer that he wants to hear is no.

Away from work—though he never gets far from it—Goldwyn can relax and be a charming and even a humorous conversationalist. Consciously humorous, that is. Not long ago he gave a luncheon at the studio for one of his writers who was going into the Army.

The high point of the occasion was a short but touching speech by Sam himself, in which he told the writer how much every one was going to miss him, and how—when it was all over—he could come back and find his old job waiting for him as always. It was a heartfelt speech, and there was hardly a dry eye in the house as Sam sat down. In the moment of hushed silence just before some one remembered to applaud, Sam looked across the table at the writer he'd been addressing. "Of course," he said dryly, "you have a contract to that effect."

Laugh Not On Sam

The laugh is no longer always on Sam. After all, there isn't anything funny about turning out successful motion pictures for thirty-one years. Ten years ago Will Rogers, addressing the Academy Award banquet, had the hot shots of the industry rolling in the aisles with Goldwyn jokes when he stopped short.

"Well," he drawled, "we all joke about Sam, but I'll say this—if a lot of you birds knew anywhere near as much about the motion-picture business as Sam, you'd be sitting a lot prettier than you are now."

And that still goes.

Billion-Dollar Orange Squeeze

by Dickson Hartwell

By 1946 orange juice was taken for granted by the grandchildren of those to whom the Christmas-stocking orange had been a big treat. Here is how it all came about.

Many an American dreams of the day he can retire and own an orange grove in California. Being a citrus grower can be a soft life. Believe it or not, he can have his trees sprayed, his crop picked, the fruit washed, graded, and packed, shipped to market, and get the cash for it without lifting a finger.

He can, that is, if he is lucky enough to find citrus-growing land at a reasonable price (try it sometime!) and becomes a member of the California Fruit Growers Exchange, one of the most amazing outfits of its kind.

Three fourths of all citrus growers in California and Arizona belong to the Exchange. Actually, it's just a lot of relatively little growers organized into one whopping big marketing co-operative which has the power and resources of a vast corporation. This year it will have handled citrus fruit worth $350,000,000 at retail.

Behind this impersonal statistic is a dazzling tale of human ingenuity and enterprise which boosted the average yearly consumption of oranges from 25 a person to 125, and it's still going up.

The big boost was sparked in 1915 when the Exchange, with its usual eye to benefiting its members, discovered that you could "drink an orange." It was a discovery as important to the citrus industry as the invention of the cotton gin was to the South. It was based on the simple theory that a man could "drink" three times as many oranges as he could eat.

This squeeze deal has sold at least a billion dollars' worth of fruit under the famous copyrighted name Sunkist.

The idea behind this organization was simply one of survival! It was born fifty years ago when Western citrus growers faced the prospect of starving to death beneath fruit-laden trees. Unscrupulous agents handled the crop then, and in such a way that the growers inevitably came out on the losing end.

Today, with its 14,500 member growers, the Exchange is busily engaged in making citrus growing as pleasantly free as possible from toil and care, without diminishing either the size or the certainty of the financial return.

Growers do not belong directly to the marketing co-operative itself, but to the local packing-house associations. As a member of a packing-house unit the grower agrees that the Exchange may have all his crop. There are 206 such units, which belong, in turn, to some twenty-five district exchanges. The district units elect one member to serve in the top organization—the Exchange. This type of federated co-operative gives the grower help where he needs it most—on his grove.

Last year Exchange growers averaged $2.74 a box for their oranges, which made them very happy. (This is the price on the tree; the same oranges cost the consumer $7.50.) But oranges have at times gone begging for fifty cents a box, and conservative growers figure a probable average return of one dollar a box.

Good groves—and some do much better—average 500 boxes to the acre. A twenty-acre grove, the minimum recommended size, should therefore gross $10,000 a year. Irrigation, fertilization, pest control, and similar incidentals bring that down to $6,600, and a further cut is taken for interest of 6 per cent on the $60,000 investment required in normal times for a producing grove of this size. This slices the grower's net to $3,000, which will be further reduced by labor costs for work he doesn't do himself. Understand, these are figures for the long pull. At today's prices a grower who bought such a grove before the war can readily *net* $10,000, and many larger groves are producing $40,000 to $50,000 a year net.

The prospect of any Johnny-come-lately enjoying the traditional life of ease and prosperity in the California citrus belt in the near future is, unfortunately, somewhat remote. There is almost no good citrus land left in California, and what there is costs $2,000 or more an acre, or just twice what old-timers say it is worth.

Prices for producing groves have hit $7,000 an acre and the end is not yet in sight. Marginal groves can be purchased for one third that sum, but experienced growers say most of them shouldn't be taken as a gift. Labor, which formerly was available in quantity at fifty cents an hour, is now a dollar and scarce. Nursery stock—young trees ready to set out which will begin paying for themselves in five years—is costing up to $4.50 a tree, while normally the best sold for $1.50. The trees will bear for twenty-five or thirty years, though, in good, properly cared-for soil.

Normal expenditures for cultural care now run Exchange members $168 an acre a year, but these costs can climb up to $300 an acre without much trouble. For example, last winter more than one grower burned 10,000 gallons of oil as a smudge protection from frost at four cents a gallon.

Dynamic President

Credited with contributing mightily to the potency of the Fruit Growers Exchange is dynamic 73-year-old Charles C. Teague, who has been its president since 1920. For nearly thirty years Teague also has been president of Limon-

In 1915 The California Fruit Growers Exchange discovered that "you could drink an orange" and parlayed that knowledge into a billion dollar industry. Here debutantes pick oranges.

eria, the world's largest lemon-ranch. His own ranch covers 3,800 acres and provides 400 homes for as many workers. The payroll runs to more than $75,000 a month and the ranch is capitalized at $2,500,000.

Soft spoken but demanding action, Teague is blessed with an insatiable, relentless curiosity. His investigations have resulted in improved orchard heaters (without which there could be no California citrus industry), methods of storage and packing which prevent fruit spoilage, and the elimination of a virulent infectious citrus plague known as poison rot. One time when he couldn't get answers fast enough, he offered a reward of $5,000 to anyone who would tell him how to build a better grove heater. Once, Italy supplied 70 per cent of all U. S. consumed lemons. Teague and other Exchange lemon growers made competition so hot that Italy was forced to withdraw from the U. S. and Canadian markets.

Although Teague is as active as ever in Exchange affairs, such leadership as there is in this democratically operated organization he shares with Paul S. Armstrong, who as general manager has responsibility for carrying out policies and decisions reached by the Exchange board in its weekly meetings. Co-operatives, Armstrong says, are the only present means by which small operators can enjoy the efficiency of a large corporation. But he adds, "They're only good when they work."

Business men like to illustrate their accounts of American enterprise with the story of how the Standard Oil Company, to develop a market for kerosene, designed and sold thousands of cheap lamps to the Chinese. This was a piddling promotion, however, compared with the way the Exchange put the squeeze on oranges by designing and selling at cost hundreds of thousands of cheap glass hand-juicers and thereby opened up a market for countless billions of oranges.

But first the Exchange had to sell the idea that oranges were more than ornaments. It wasn't so long ago that oranges were strictly a luxury item. In the old days the orange in a child's Christmas stocking was usually the only orange the child got throughout the year. No one knows how oranges got started on the breakfast table, but the custom of serving half a grapefruit at breakfast probably paved the way for the establishment of the practice of cutting an orange in two as a greeting for the new day.

Orange juice is canned for overseas shipment.

Special Spoon

The California Fruit Growers Exchange was painfully aware that the average teaspoon was an instrument of the devil when applied to half an orange. To alleviate this condition the Exchange undertook its first great promotion program. It had the International Silver Company design an orange spoon, one sufficiently narrow and sharp edged to fit an orange section neatly and dig it out with a minimum of squirting.

In 1912 this notable advance in table-surgery design was offered as the feature of a fifty-piece Orange Blossom-pattern silverware set. The spoon could be had for ten cents and wrappers from Sunkist oranges. Distribution of spoons alone went to 5,000 a day.

During the five years this offer was plugged nobody now knows how many million pieces of silver were distributed, but the Exchange became International Silver's largest customer. The deal was stopped only because of a revolution in the citrus business—orange juice.

At that time growers were already producing more oranges than the public would eat laboriously by hand. Americans were accustomed to lemonade, but the idea of drinking plain orange juice was novel. The only juice extractors in use were too small to be handy, being designed for lemons.

The exchange promptly designed an effective glass household reamer, put it on the market for a dime, and in a few months sold the first 600,000 of a total of over 3,000,000. Manufacturers took notice and introduced other models. The Exchange designed electric extractors and sold 88,000 of them to restaurants and drugstores, again at cost. Electric models for home use were developed by the Exchange and nearly 200,000 of them sold. Pretty nearly everybody had some gadget that would take juice out of an orange. All they needed was the oranges. They bought them by the thousands of carloads, and still do.

Dovetailing with its more spectacular promotions is a remarkable system of distribution. The Exchange freight bill is $60,000,000 a year, and to get the fruit to the right market in the best condition is a man-size job.

Marketing System

The Exchange has offices in fifty-seven cities connected by telegraph or teletype which report constantly on the state of the market in their territory. If a couple of extra carloads of Florida oranges arrive unexpectedly in Des Moines, for example, temporarily glutting the market, the Exchange can send any fruit it might have en route to Des Moines to another city where the demand is greater than the supply. This can be done anywhere in the country any day in the year, with any one of the 100,000 freight cars the Exchange ships annually. No privately operated system of marketing perishables on a national scale anywhere else in the world can equal this in size or efficiency. Its beneficial effect on all citrus producers, in addition to Exchange members, is obvious.

The backbone of its sales program, the Exchange claims, is its advertising. Its advertising has been so potent, in fact, that the Exchange is credited today with making southern California a little Iowa simply because back in 1907 its first advertising was tested there. With only $10,000 to spend for the whole campaign—that would last about one day now—the Exchange teamed up with the Southern Pacific and enticed the susceptible Iowans with an alluring slogan, "Oranges for Health—California for Wealth." Orange sales jumped ahead 300 per cent faster in Iowa than in the rest of the country and hundreds of farmers entrained for the land of sunshine.

Research On Citrus

The Exchange and its advertising agency have been together nearly forty years in what some observers say is the longest such honeymoon in American business. Constant needling by Charles Teague and a few other farsighted growers kept up Exchange advertising even when oranges were down to forty cents a box. Now the Exchange is spending around $3,000,000 a year for advertising. It is raised by current assessments of seven cents a box for oranges, fourteen cents for lemons, and one cent for grapefruit.

Exchange advertising claims have been models of temperance—in part, doubtless, because of the restraining influence of the organization's own research division, which has spent some $3,000,000 investigating all phases of its business from growing and packing-house methods to new products and nutrition.

As long as twenty-three years ago the Exchange was collecting evidence developed by the University of California that an orange added to the diet of school children through the midmorning lunch produced a greater weight gain than half a pint of milk given at the same period. The gain was in fact 141 per cent greater than anticipated by the researchers. These astonishing results would have been an excellent basis for an advertising campaign.

But the Exchange merely reprinted the results of the study and sent them to teachers and interested groups.

Even more remarkable is a clause inserted by the Exchange in the agreement covering each project it supports. This gives the research institution the right to publish the results whether they are favorable or unfavorable to citrus fruits.

The Exchange has supported numerous studies such as the effect of orange juice's vitamin C on tuberculosis, the effect of orange and lemon juice on tooth decay (in which study 450 children participated for a year at a cost to the Exchange of $50,000), and the effect of citrus on poliomyelitis, rheumatic fever, and arthritis. War studies included speeding up wound healing with vitamin C and the effect of lemon substances in aiding combat pilots against high-altitude lung hemorrhage.

But while the grower is benefited from such activities, they seem somewhat remote from his day-to-day living. He accepts such long-term research objectives because he has faith in the Exchange. But he gets more immediate effect, he feels, from the Sunkist service men who make 100,000 calls a year on retail dealers and arrange for huge displays that will send eager housewives home from shopping with bags full of oranges. He likes the Exchange distribution of some 2,000,000 educational booklets a year to teachers and dietitians, even though they don't contain a single plug for Sunkist. He is also mildly approving of the twenty-two motion pictures the Exchange has produced for which there are annual audiences of 1,000,000.

It is natural, though, that the grower would be most appreciative of his Exchange membership when the crew from the packing house comes to spray his trees or pick his fruit. His crop isn't harvested all at once. Oranges stay ripe on the trees for months and the Exchange packing houses pick only a portion of the crop at a time, thereby maintaining a steady flow to the market and preventing alternate gluts and shortages and wildcat fluctuations in price. It appeals particularly to the grower that his fruit is kept separate from all others until it is carefully graded. By thus subtly making it pay to grow the best, the Exchange has put a premium on quality to which growers have responded with enthusiasm.

Although some California farmers also have citrus trees, most growers are not even fourth cousins to dirt farmers. The one-crop grower has no onerous farm chores, his workday begins at seven and ends at four or five.

Citrus growing is no proposition for a dullwit. For $60,000 worth of citrus offers no less responsibilities than a hardware store, garage, or wholesale house of equal size. But the Exchange has certainly minimized the risks not only for its members but for all growers. And the prospective grower wondering about the future can be sure it will soon have us squeezing another billion oranges.

Citrus Fair held in California, 1895.

Sunkist Oranges
Trail
Sunkist

The Future of the Atom

by Oscar Schisgall

Dr. J. Robert Oppenheimer discussed for an interviewer at the end of 1945 the coming of the Atomic Age and what it could mean for mankind.

"It is quite feasible that a city the size of Seattle should be completely heated from an atomic energy source in less than five years. Of course it will take much longer for the full technological benefits of atomic power to make themselves felt."

Dr. J. Robert Oppenheimer, who had been in charge of the atomic bomb's research and development laboratories at Los Alamos, New Mexico, spoke without excitement. He is a quiet man, with the scientist's precise, unimpassioned manner of stating facts.

We were alone in his office. He paced the floor and puffed at a pipe while he talked—thin, loose-limbed, wearing casual brown tweeds. The first sprinklings of gray are already visible in his hair. I knew, of course, that he had long ago achieved an eminent reputation in physics, and that his work at the University of California had been widely recognized and quoted; nevertheless, until I met him, I marveled at the fact that anyone so young—he is forty-one—should have been given the tremendous responsibility of guiding and co-ordinating the work of some 600 of the world's most distinguished scientists.

His confidence, his precision, the clarity of his ideas make you understand at once why he was chosen for the task that was brought to such historic completion over Hiroshima. When talking of atomic energy, he becomes intense. His eyes, his hands, his whole body join in emphasizing the points he makes. And he makes points which few others have brought to public attention, especially in discussing the peacetime possibilities of the world's new source of power.

"People ask," he said, "how soon, if at all, we will be able to control atomic energy so that we may devote it to commercial use. They ask if the explosive properties of the atomic bomb can be reduced to a gradual controlled flow of power which will serve humanity rather than destroy it. The facts are almost the reverse of this process of reasoning."

He stopped pacing the floor and pointed his pipe at me.

Bomb Was End Result

"The atomic bomb," he said, "was not a step on the road to the production of controlled atomic energy. The bomb itself was the end result, the solution of a military problem that had been given to us. In coping with that problem we learned how to create and control atomic energy a year and a half before Hiroshima. But we had to pass that point. *We had to find ways to make that energy explode.* The production of atomic energy was merely a step on the way to that goal.

"Of course we produced this energy at a low temperature. We had no time to pause and develop it. With a pressing war job to do, we had to neglect other avenues of progress in order to produce the bomb as quickly as possible. Now that the military goal has been achieved, however, there is no reason why we cannot return to the further development of atomic energy as we learned to create it a year and a half ago."

Here was a revelation that brought the commercial uses of atomic energy much nearer than most of us had supposed. I could not help commenting on the spur the war had given to scientific accomplishment—in the field of radar, for instance; in aviation; in the development of high-power fuels; and specifically in the production of the atomic bomb. Dr. Oppenheimer, however, had views of his own about this.

Robert Oppenheimer: "Uses for atomic energy are infinite. We can't even guess at them!"

"It's true," he said, "that the bomb was a great technical achievement, but in many ways it set science *back* five years. So many men devoted themselves to this one project that other work in their fields had to be neglected. This was their part in the war; they concentrated on it all of their time and thought and strength. It was inevitable that other fundamental research should suffer during those years. That loss will have to be added to the cost of the war.

"And science sustained another blow, too. You speak of developing atomic energy for commercial purposes. Such development requires competently trained men. But as a result of the war, science faces a serious deficit in such men.

"For the past few years our college students have gone into the armed forces. No deferments were granted to science students. The most competent teachers, too, were taken out of the universities to solve wartime problems. We had to win the war; all of us understood that and accepted it. Still, we now have to confront the facts that, first, we have a lack of trained students—the scientists of tomorrow—whose ranks it will take several years to replenish and, second, that the present generation of scientists has had to abandon the field of fundamental research in order to do its part in the war. So you see why I say that in many ways science has *lost* several years of progress."

To continue work on the bomb itself, it became clear as we talked, holds little further interest for Dr. Oppenheimer. It is a task that is finished, behind him. It is time to turn again to fundamental research in the laboratory.

I mentioned current theories about a pea-sized pellet of atomic energy that would soon run a refrigerator for ten years, or furnish endless power to an automobile, or keep a furnace working for a decade. Dr. Oppenheimer did not smile.

Not For Home Use

"From what we have so far learned," he said, "it is a mistake to speak of having atomic energy run your car, power your airplane or your motorboat. Atomic energy, as we know it now, is not feasible for such purposes or for private home use. It can be employed only on a large scale—for tremendous industrial installations or for the needs of an entire community. What you say about the amount of energy that can be concentrated in a pea-sized pellet is true. But the release of that energy now requires at least a fifty-ton unit. The unit must be encased in walls of concrete many feet thick; these are necessary shields against the radiation generated in the process of releasing atomic energy. Therefore, it would hardly be practical, without some new invention, to speak of employing such units in the home or in automobiles.

"If, however, you wish to distribute power to a whole community from a central atomic source, that *is* possible. A community can readily accommodate a large unit. You may even build such a unit into a great ocean ship. But you would hardly build it into a private yacht. We face limitations at present which we must recognize.

"Still, there are many things we already know we can do. To these we can turn at once. The production of heat or of electric power for whole communities is one of them."

"Would such a change necessitate the rebuilding of present equipment in the home?" I asked.

"The need for alterations will be surprisingly slight," Dr. Oppenheimer said. "Atomic energy will not supplant present home equipment; it will merely change the source of its power. It means a change of fuel, not of system; an atomic energy unit instead of a conventional boiler. It will probably work out that the new source of power will not supplant coal and oil but will supplement them and make possible operations which are not dreamed of today."

The things Dr. Oppenheimer said, as well as his factual manner of saying them, seemed to bring the atomic age to the immediate present. He was not discussing theories; he was talking of existing conditions. Because of this, perhaps, I reverted to a statement he had made earlier in our conversation.

"When atomic energy was first released, a year and a half ago," I asked, "how hot did your systems run?"

"Not very," he said. "Not hot enough for any practical purposes. Just enough, let us say, to keep a pot of breakfast coffee warm. But the principle for obtaining such heat was established. We did not develop it further because that was not our problem at the time. Now people will have the leisure to take up that principle again and to apply it to peacetime needs."

Robert Oppenheimer and General Groves after the first test of the atomic bomb at Alamagordo.

(Top) in 1950 Dr. Vannevar Bush (center) World War II scientist told reporters "it will take more than atom bomb to stop Soviet." (Bottom) site of first atom bomb tests.

"Is there danger in the necessary research? Danger for the men engaged in it?"

"There is danger, yes, but in the laboratory, of course, we take every possible precaution against it. During our three years of work at Los Alamos we had only one fatality. The danger lies principally in the radiation that surrounds our experimental units. And yet this very radioactivity is a by-product of our work that can be of inestimable value to science; particularly to medicine, since it provides new fields for research in radiotherapy."

Dr. Oppenheimer paced the floor again while he discussed the therapeutic potentialities that lie in atomic energy. He spoke of them for several minutes. Then he stopped, and the tone of his voice changed.

"The truth is," he said, "that we cannot consider atomic energy merely in its industrial or military sense. Its possible uses are infinite. With our restricted imaginations we cannot even guess at them. The same could have been said, I think, of every new principle for producing power that man ever discovered.

"Could Faraday, for example, foresee the total effect of electrical power on civilization? Could he foresee its economic, its social, its cultural, its scientific results? In his day he could not even imagine them. And when the internal-combustion engine came into existence, could it be foreseen that because of it airplanes would some day be possible? For the same reason—the limiting factor of human imagination—we cannot predict today what atomic energy will mean to the future in technological change, in the evolution of science, or even in the philosophy of man. So far, we know only that we have produced a new source of power, and that, within certain feasible areas, we can soon begin to put it to work."

Common Danger, Interest

Since this power had been developed at Los Alamos by scientists who represented several nations, we came to a discussion of the political future of atomic energy.

"Not only is it an international problem," Dr. Oppenheimer said, "but this, I think, is one of its greatest hopes. It should result in new conceptions of national and international welfare.

No nation can hope to hold a monopoly an a form of energy. Nor is any one nation, including our own, wholly responsible for what we know today of atomic energy. The background of our present knowledge was supplied by scientists from every country of Europe and many elsewhere. Of course we are glad that the atomic bomb was developed in the United States. But we recognize the fact that ours were the final steps in a long series of advances made in past years.

"But that is not really the main point. Atomic weapons are very terrible weapons; the mixed awe and revulsion which all of us felt was a proper feeling. Before our children are grown to manhood the weapons can be made far more terrible, in vast numbers, at a cost small compared to the costs of war as we have known it. There is the deadliest danger for all mankind in an atomic armament race; there is the greatest common need there has ever been for all nations to collaborate in an effective prevention of war. On this one point almost all of us who have worked on the atomic bomb are unanimous—this, even more than the possible contribution toward shortening the war, was the reason we felt it so desperately necessary to get the job done, the facts proven, in all their terror and urgency, for the world to see.

"Our hope for the future is to see this new form of energy as the peril, the challenge, and the hope that it really is. It can bring about a major change in human life. Here, if we are wise, is a force we can apply to forge the peoples of the earth into closer unity, for in it they will see a new common danger, a new common interest, a new commonwealth. I hope we shall have the wisdom and the courage to use this new power."

1945 meeting on controlling the use of atomic bombs is presided over by President Truman.

How to Break into Fort Knox

by Stacy V. Jones

The biggest caper of all would be stealing the gold at Fort Knox. Readers of this 1949 article learned why it could not be done.

Hold a nation-wide contest among safe-crackers with the worst criminal records, and pick a crew of the most expert. Then invite them for a week-end at the Fort Knox gold depository in Kentucky. Send away all the guards Saturday noon and shoo off the soldiery, so as to give the boys a free hand with their drills and nitroglycerin. Come back at 9 A. M. Monday—and officials of the Mint predict that the cracksmen guests still won't be inside the vault.

Of course the Bureau of the Mint has no intention of staging such a party. Indeed, there is probably no building in the country where visitors are less welcome.

Everybody knows about the treasure at Fort Knox. The girl whose mother used to say, "I wouldn't marry you for a king's ransom," now says, "I wouldn't marry you for all the gold in Fort Knox." And almost everybody would like to get a glimpse of the $12½ billions in gold bullion which it holds. But nobody gets in except Treasury officials, the rare fellow who has business there, and an occasional V.I.P.I. (Very Important Person Indeed).

Almost daily the Treasury Department in Washington receives a letter saying the writer is going to Kentucky on a trip, and asking for a pass to the gold depository. All anybody gets is a chance to glimpse the building from the Dixie Highway, 30 miles southwest of Louisville, or from one of the roads in the military reservation.

The Fort Knox treasure house stands on a gently sloping hill, which gives the guards a clear view in all directions. It is surrounded by a high steel fence, floodlighted at night. Inside the fence and outside each corner of the building is a pillbox from which a guard can shoot along two sides of the building. These little turrets can be entered only from inside the depository. If need be, a guard can hole up in his turret indefinitely, with his own food, water, and heat. At each side of the gate in the steel fence is a sentry box like the turrets.

Tourists Unwelcome

From Dixie Highway the depository looks like a large tomb. It is, indeed, a mausoleum for gold. No signs direct visitors to it; quite the reverse. If you turn off the highway onto Bullion Boulevard, one of the reservation roads, you will see a sign with the rather ominous inscription: "Danger. Keep Out. Armed Guard. U. S. Treasury Dept. Bullion Depository." Then, if you turn into the driveway, the first thing you see is exactly the kind of traffic sign that keeps you from driving the wrong way into a one-way street: "Do Not Enter."

Anybody who persists, as I did the other day, finds on his right the greeting: "*HALT*. State Your Business in Loud Speaker. *DO NOT ENTER* Without Permission." You are still a good 100 yards from the gate. A voice says civilly from the loud-speaker, "State your business." If you're a tourist or a wandering reporter and say so, that ends it. You don't get any further.

In my own case, Fort Knox headquarters later vouched for my credentials and introduced me by telephone to the depository's captain of the guard, W. L. Jenkins, who granted me permission to drive up to the gate and look at the building from there. On this closer approach, I discovered a further sign near the gate: "Stop on Red Signal." As the signal wasn't red, I kept on, and parked. Master Sergeant Lyle H. Beardsley accompanied me from Fort Knox headquarters, and the view was a treat for him too: it was the closest he had got in three years' duty on the reservation. We walked along the fence and chatted with a guard in a sentry box who would not commit himself on anything but the weather.

The signs and loud-speaker are effective defense against tourists. So far, the only near-invasions have been by several drunks who had lost their way and approached the fence from the side. The depository guards called M.P.s from the fort to dispose of them. Then there was one valiant lady tourist who walked up and poked a camera between the fence bars. No unauthorized person has actually got inside the fence.

If anything really menacing approached, the guards could call help, in a matter of minutes, from the 29,000 troops on the surrounding military reservation of Fort Knox proper.

Once a legitimate visitor is admitted through the gate, he proceeds to the front door, under surveillance from the pillboxes and sentry boxes. The front door is double. After he is admitted through the first, it is locked behind him, and he must identify himself to the guards before he is admitted to the building through a second door.

A burglar's problems would really begin inside the second door. The vault is like a treasure chest enclosed in a trunk, with its own walls and ceilings. (Here, of course, I am forced to rely on descriptions by Treasury officials, for no reporter has been admitted to the temple of gold.) Our burglar finds himself, then, in a high corridor between the granite-and-concrete wall of the building and the reinforced-concrete casing of the vault, which is 25 inches thick.

Before him is the door to the vault itself. This little object, which is made of special steel, weighs 26 tons. The only way to open it is for two men to work combinations, one after another. It won't open then if the time

"Gold Bullion Depository" at Fort Knox kentucky, under construction in July 1936.

lock is on. As the vault doesn't need to be opened every day, the guard who sets the time lock doesn't set it for any regular hour, and he doesn't even tell the other guards what hour he selects.

Oxyacetylene torches would have little effect on the door or walls, as copper strips embedded in them would carry away the heat. Electric drills and hacksaws likewise would barely scratch them. The vault casing includes steel plates, steel I-beams, and steel cylinders laced with hoop bands and encased in concrete. The roof of the vault is just as tough as the sides, and there would be no privacy for a cracksman boring from the top: guards in the corridors could see him through mirrors.

Any fumbling about inside the building would set off alarms. The Mint has installed the usual watchmen's signals that banks use, also others it doesn't care to discuss. Microphones pick up conversations in the vault so they can be heard in the guardroom. Every watchman's report is recorded by machinery on a paper which falls into a special locked safe, so that if he makes an error he cannot cover it up. Any opening of the door of the big vault is recorded in the same way.

In addition to telephone connections with headquarters on the military reservation next door and with the police in Louisville, the depository has a short-wave set for emergency use in case its wires should be cut. There is also a siren. It has its own water supply and its own power plant for light and heat. Besides gunfire, it has gas weapons and protection against gas attack.

If the regular communications between headquarters and the depository are interrupted, a platoon of heavily armed soldiers shows up outside the fence and asks, in military terms, what gives. There is a secret system to prevent the soldiers from being fooled by fav-

Upon completion $6,000,000,000 in gold was stored in suspended subterranean vaults.

orable reports given under duress.

Bombproof Vault

The Fort Knox depository is small for so important a building. The courthouse back in your home county is probably larger, but not nearly so solid. It was built in 1936, on land formerly part of the military reservation, at a cost of $560,000 and was made bombproof, at least for those pre-atomic days.

Trucks containing gold shipment for Fort Knox are guarded as they leave the Treasury office.

The popular crack that "they dig gold out of the ground at one place and then bury it again at Fort Knox" is partly true, because the vault has two floors, and one of them is below ground level. The vault, which, like the building around it, was designed to be bombproof, measures 40 by 60 feet. It has 28 compartments for gold storage, 14 on each level.

In the compartments are about 12,500 tons of gold, all in bar form, a ton being worth roughly a million dollars at the official price of $35 an ounce. Each bar is somewhat smaller than a building brick, but would be harder to throw, as it weighs about 27½ pounds. It's worth $14,000.

Between the infrequent shipments, the vault door is opened occasionally for inspection and to prevent "freezing." It fits so snugly in its frame that if left undisturbed for a long period the slight accumulation of rust might cause it to stick and refuse to open. Each compartment in which gold is stored has its individual door that is locked and sealed. A compartment which was opened a few months ago for an inspection by John W. Snyder, Secretary of the Treasury, hadn't been unlocked for two years.

The compartment seals are officially examined from time to time, to verify that the gold is there. In debate some years ago, a senator remarked, "We take it for granted that the gold is still in Kentucky. If it is not and nobody should find it out, that would not make any difference." President Roosevelt once made an inspection of the depository.

A number of U. S. senators have visited the building, including President Truman when he was a senator. Representatives can also enter, after clearance with Washington, but seldom do. Generals hardly ever get inside.

Registered Mail

The Treasury ships gold the way you and I might do it—by registered mail. The Post Office Department supplies postal inspectors, and the Treasury assigns Secret Service men to the shipping points and arranges for troops to travel on the special trains used. At Fort Knox heavy military guards are thrown around the precious mail. The postage on $5 or $6 billions runs to about $1 million.

As the bars of gold are of almost pure form, they are soft and must be handled with the greatest care to avoid loss through abrasion.

Contrary to popular opinion, the whole gold hoard is not at Knox. Nor is any of it in the Treasury Building at Washington. Indeed, there's not an ounce of gold in the capital vaults, unless you include jewelry and keepsakes that American citizens in foreign countries have confided to embassies and consulates over the years. But $11½ billions of the gold treasure is in depositories at New York, Denver, San Francisco, Philadelphia, and Seattle. The biggest deposit outside Fort Knox is in Denver, which has $5.7 billions. Early in the war, when there was fear of an invasion of the Pacific coast, bullion was shipped to Denver from San Francisco and Seattle. The depositories are all fortified, although none but Fort Knox has troops next door.

Bullion would be awkward to steal and virtually impossible to sell in this country. This may be one reason Mrs. Ross carries her vast responsibility with equanimity.

Melted gold is poured into steel molds.

Background of the Bomb

by Oscar Schisgall

Now it could be told. Two months after the atom bomb devastated Hiroshima on August 6, 1945, Oscar Schisgall told how General Groves and his men kept the astounding secret.

Though 99 may sound strange as a name for a man, hundreds of people throughout the country have learned to accept it quite naturally as the pseudonym of Major General Leslie Richard Groves, chief of the atomic-bomb project. Three years ago, when he began traveling about the country to select sites and supervise construction for the fantastic venture, he was referred to by the code name of "G. G." In New York, however, a nearsighted telegraph operator misread the initials and relayed them as 99. The error caused a day of confusion; but the confusion subsided quickly and the number stuck.

That is perhaps the simplest bit of unconventionality about an enterprise which, from the start, operated in a degree of secrecy never before attempted or maintained, for as long as three years, with such consummate success. In the end the only thing powerful enough to shatter it was the atomic bomb that fell on Hiroshima.

Historians may regard that particular bomb or the one which blasted Nagasaki a few days later as the immediate cause of Japan's surrender. But some fifty men—and one woman—will tell you that the bomb which really defeated Japan exploded on July 16, 1945, in the badlands of New Mexico. That was the day of the first and only test the atomic bomb ever had. For three years some 300,000 people had labored toward this climactic morning, and when it finally came nobody knew whether the bomb would work.

"We had two billion dollars and scores of reputations staked on that moment," General Groves said. We were in his Washington office the day after the Hiroshima blast. He sounded tired. A heavy man, he leaned back in his chair, staring at his desk as if seeing all the events of three years pass in review. "That last day, while we waited for the explosion, brought a good many of our men as close to nervous breakdowns as they'll ever be. I'm not a betting man, but I must say that in a way it was like betting on a horse race when you're not at the track. All you can do is wait at a telephone, without seeing anything, to hear whether your horse has come in."

"It Works! It Works!"

The general and some fifty of the world's leading scientists—all of them key men in the venture—were gathered on the edge of the badlands twenty miles from the spot where the bomb would or would not explode. The controls for the test were hidden deep in a

General Groves, who ran the atomic bomb project, in 1945.

General Groves and his assistant General Thomas Farrell iron out problems only days before the atomic bomb was dropped on Hiroshima.

near-by dugout, with troops everywhere on guard. Overhead, at 35,000 feet, a B-29 flew out to make aerial observations. Tension had reached its climax—and then, to everyone's dismay, a thunderstorm arrived to delay the test for two interminable hours.

That was the point at which Dr. J. Robert Oppenheimer, who had been in charge of laboratory work, lost all academic reserve. He began to pace back and forth, nervous, muttering. General Groves put an arm around his shoulder and walked with him, doing his best to calm the scientist. In fact, all who were there agree it was the general—the man with the most to gain or lose in the next two hours—who seemed the calmest of the group.

Sir James Chadwick, Britain's most celebrated nuclear physicist, who won the Nobel prize for proving the neutron's existence, has a reputation for unusual composure. He is austere, cold. But when at last the blast occurred, his austerity deserted him. He became as exuberant as all the others and ran about repeating the cry that came from everyone else: "It works! It works!"

Oddly, those seem to be the only words the witnesses of the blast can recall hearing.

The telephone lines to Washington at once carried the announcement: *"New York Yankees"*—the prearranged code signal to report "Successful beyond expectations." The code had been based on the names of big-league baseball clubs. Had the experiment ended in utter failure, the words "Cincinnati Reds" would have gone to Washington. "Below expectations" would have been "Cleveland Indians." "As expected" would have been "Brooklyn Dodgers."

Sitting with the man most responsible for the triumph, you cannot help marveling at his calm. Those who had worked with him for three years had told me he'd always been calm —even on July 16. "He just *had* to be levelheaded," one of his assistants said. "You spend three years with some of the world's top scientists, trying to referee their conflicting opinions, and if your decisions are to be intelligent, you've got to be calm. Put three experts to work on a problem—a chemist, a mathematician, and a nuclear physicist—and the chances are you'll get not only three different approaches to a solution but even three different solutions. Again and again the general had to make his choice or to compromise among those solutions. He had to get the best out of them all. You can't leave a job like that to a man who tends to become excited."

Rare Qualifications

Major General Groves is a big man with a gray mustache and thick graying hair. As we talked, his voice was low. The movements of his massive figure, especially of his hands, were almost languid. Yet the languor, I know, must be deceptive. A languid man couldn't have been on an Army football team. A languid man couldn't play tennis the way the general plays it. Even now, at forty-eight, he faces some of America's ranking players in his Sunday games.

Tennis is the only recreation for which he has found time in these last three years. And he has made a fine player of his sixteen-year-old daughter, Gwen, who appears destined for major tournaments.

Three years ago Leslie Richard Groves was an Army engineer, with the temporary rank of colonel. He had led his West Point class in engineering and had achieved a reputation in construction down in Nicaragua; he had added to that reputation when the Army brought him back to the States. The atomic-bomb project was going to need a construction expert. Moreover, it was going to need a man who could co-ordinate problems of abstract science, construction, engineering, labor, and industry—one who could talk the language of each group. Not many men in America meet such diverse qualifications.

Groves was summoned to the White House. He went with General Marshall and the Secretary of War. When he left he carried the most stupendous assignment the President could have given any man—to supervise, in all its bewildering ramifications, the creation of an atomic bomb.

Had President Roosevelt believed that the undertaking would succeed?

The late President, General Groves assured me, had been completely confident. The President loved excitement. This was exactly the kind of venture that could stir his imagination

This is Alamagordo, New Mexico, where first atomic bomb tests took place in July 1945.

and rouse his enthusiasm. From the start he gave Groves virtual carte blanche. The Secretary of War and General Marshall left all technical decisions to the Groves office. And President Truman continued that policy.

One Woman Did Much

Then the general said something astonishing. He tossed the words out almost casually as he nodded to the young woman who shares his office.

"Few people know how many of our decisions were made by my executive officer here, Mrs. O'Leary. I haven't talked about it, because people just won't believe one woman could have done so much."

Jean O'Leary's desk stands a few feet from the general's. She smiles at you, and you are stunned by the idea that this crisp, competent, exceedingly attractive young woman has for three years been the general's executive officer, with the reins of the entire atomic-bomb project often placed in her hands. With the exception of the small policy committee, she and the general are the only two people who, from the beginning, had their eyes on every facet of the tremendous undertaking. This office—particularly her desk—was the central switchboard through which all reports, all communications flowed. Ninety per cent of the papers and oral information that came to this office, the general said, were "top secret." Jean O'Leary handled them all. She insists she is not a scientist. Yet she knows better than does anyone else in America, save the general himself, all the struggles, all the troubles, all the aspirations that went into the making of the atomic bomb.

The general refers to her as "Jol"—a name coined from her initials. He merely smiles in a wise way if you point out that other generals' executive officers are military men, usually colonels. In this civilian woman he has found the ultimate in the kind of efficiency, competence, and reliability he needed.

She began as his secretary five years ago, immediately after her husband died. When the general took on the job of producing an atomic bomb, she became his administrative officer and plunged with him into the task of organizing the 300,000 people, building the widely scattered plants in Tennessee, New Mexico, and Washington, and managing the army of scientists and technicians the project required. Like the general, she worked without reference to the clock, day or night, seven days a week. She needed work like that, she confessed, to help her face her bereavement. But at the same time it created a problem in the rearing of her daughter, Connie, now fourteen. You know, however, as you study her alert face, that she must have solved that problem, too.

"How did *you* react to the strain of July 16?" I asked Mrs. O'Leary. "Were you as nervous as the others?"

"I was quite calm," she said. "The only thing I did wrong that morning was to tear up a hundred and eighty red ration stamps and toss them away!"

Unusual Secrecy

The fact that President Roosevelt never underestimated the enormousness of the task to which he had assigned General Groves was amply proved by the caliber of the policy committee he appointed to work with the general. Besides General Marshall and Secretary of War Stimson, there were such men as Dr. Vennevar Bush, director of the Office of Scientific Research and Development; Dr. James B. Conant, president of Harvard; Dr. Richard C. Tolman of the California Institute of Technology.

"In all," I asked, "how many men really knew what you were trying to accomplish?"

"About ten," Mrs. O'Leary answered for the general. "But about a thousand others probably suspected."

"Does the ten include Winston Churchill?"

"Yes—it includes several Englishman."

Again and again, as we talked, the secrecy which surrounded the venture loomed as one of its most amazing factors. Hundreds of distinguished scientists had to be recruited for the work, and every one of them, the general pointed out, was identified not by his own name but by a pseudonym. Thus, if Dr. Oppenheimer sent in a report, his fictitious name appeared on it. Other scientists who had to read the report could never identify its source; most of them did not even know Dr. Oppenheimer was associated with the project.

After the atomic bomb was dropped on Hiroshima General Richard Groves, shown here with his family, took a much deserved vacation.

"That, of course, was just one of many necessary precautions," the general said. "We had to have code names for everybody and everything. And those codes were constantly changed. Moreover, while I traveled—and I had to travel about a hundred thousand miles a year—my long-distance telephone conversation with the office had to be conducted not only in code but in double-talk. Mrs. O'Leary and I have become experts at double-talk."

The need for secrecy, carried to extraordinary lengths, did strange things to the general's family. Not one of them—Mrs. Groves, daughter Gwen, or son Dick, recently graduated from West Point—was aware of the job to which the general had been assigned. Mrs. Groves never visited his office. One day, when she dropped by to pick him up for dinner, she had to wait for him in an anteroom. It was her only appearance at the War Department.

Families In Dark

Since they didn't know, the family wondered. Was father merely warming a Washington chair because no job could be found for him? Son Dick wrote harried letters from West Point. What could he say to friends who asked what his father did? When your father is a major general, people want to know, at the very least, what sort of duties he performs. General Groves could give his son no answer.

Moreover, the general had to sacrifice virtually all social life. He was away from home some six months of the year. When he wasn't traveling he worked at his Washington office from 8 A. M. until 9 or 10 P. M. every day; often he stayed later. Luncheon—invariably a salad, coffee, and a slice of chocolate cake—was eaten at his desk. If he went home for dinner at all, it was only to hurry back to the office. The only relaxation he allowed himself in these three years was the Sunday sessions on the Army and Navy Club's tennis courts.

When he was out of Washington his family never knew where to reach him. Any emergency calls—even one that went to him after a death in the family—had to be relayed through the office. And at the office only Jean O'Leary knew where to find him.

Yes, indeed, father and his mysterious activities had to be taken on faith. Mrs. Groves never heard even the names of the scientists with whom her husband worked.

The same rule applied to all members of the policy committee. Their families were never informed of the project with which the men were connected. If Dr. Bush, Dr. Conant, or Dr. Tolman had to visit one of the atomic-bomb plants, their families knew only that they were away on the business of the Office of Scientific Research and Development. They, too, could be reached only through Mrs. O'Leary's office. This caused considerable perplexity and anxiety over a period of three years, but the success with which the secret was kept justified all precautions.

The blackout covered not only every man but every operation in the gigantic plan. When investigations had to be made even the F. B. I. and G-2 were excluded from the inner circle.

In their place the project developed its own intelligence division—600 carefully selected men and 200 specially trained officers. These were the watchdogs. They neglected nothing.

With such vigilance the project never had trouble of any kind with spies.

No Labor Problems

"We relied heavily on compartmentalizing," General Groves explained. "That is, every man worked within his own compartment. He knew what he needed to know to do his job—nothing more. The technician at Oak Ridge had no means of knowing his particular job was in any way connected with another in progress at Los Alamos or Pasco."

I asked approximately how many key men had been identified with the atomic bomb.

"If by key men you mean technical experts," the general said, "we have had as many as ten thousand working for us at one time. If you mean top ranking scientists from England and America, the number has varied between fifty and a hundred."

Wherever possible, these men were paid the same wages they had earned in civilian life, the theory being that no one ought either to gain or to lose because of his association with the bomb project. Unskilled labor received the standard wage of the area of employment.

Since the venture involved so many people over a period of three years, it seemed probable that at some time or other the death of a key man might delay operations or cause a break in the continuity of research. Surprisingly, this did not happen. Only one of the key figures died—Colonel Harry R. Kadlec of Chicago, a construction expert—but his death occurred months after he had finished his "compartmentalized" contribution.

Nor did labor problems bring delays. At a round-table conference the unions were asked to help a secret project in a race against time; they accepted General Groves' assurance that their compliance was essential to the winning of the war, and no labor difficulty ever retarded the work.

Speed—that was the word urged upon everyone. When an electrical engineering firm asked for a schedule of operations, General Groves replied, "Set yourself a schedule that can be met only by a miracle."

Were there technical failures or errors of judgment that caused delays? Surely in an enterprise as widespread as this, with its endless need for experiment, with its constant problems of choice of procedure, there must have been failures and frustrations without number: gadgets that failed, methods that collapsed.

"There were *no* failures," the general said. "There were merely eliminations of processes that did not work fast enough. Each elimination narrowed the field to other methods until at last a correct method was evolved."

That attitude, of course, typified the spirit that pervaded the venture from beginning to end. There could be no failure; only the need, from time to time, to find some new way to proceed. To assist him, General Groves was given the kind of authority which is the modern equivalent of a magic wand. His project had top priorities in men, materials, travel, and anything else it might require. He could—and did—commandeer whatever experts he needed in the Army and Navy, the best construction men in the country, the cream of the scientific world here and in England. With $2,000,000,000 at his disposal—and probably more, had he needed it—he had no financial obstacles. That was the sort of all-out drive it took to create the bomb.

One cannot help wondering—as several newspapermen were heard to wonder in the corridors of the War Department—what would happen if the U. S. government applied its resources with equal generosity to other human needs. Suppose billions were allocated to, say, the fight against cancer or polio; suppose the leaders of medicine throughout the world were brought together in a vast, concerted drive to vanquish such disease. If we repeat in other fields the magnitude of the procedures evolved by General Groves, is anything beyond human hope?

In looking back over these three years, the general can probably see as many moments of sadness as of triumph. When I asked about them, however, he shook his head. It was Jean O'Leary who told me a little about them—later.

"I used to feel" she said, "that the saddest days in the general's life were those when his friends slated to go overseas came in to say good-by. I knew he would have given a lot to go with them. And I knew some of them wondered just what he was doing here; nothing could even be discussed. Of course he did his best to look cheerful when they left. But those were the times I could see he wasn't too happy. And then there were the other times, when his son Dick all but begged to know what he was doing and there was no answer he could give."

The Happiest Day

"And his happiest day?" I asked. "July 16?"

"Well, no." Jean O'Leary's reply was slow and considered. "I'd say it was the day after the bombing of Hiroshima, when his son finally understood what had been going on and called from Fort Belvoir, with a great deal of pride, to congratulate his father. *That's* when you should have seen the general's eyes!"

General Groves is decorated by Secretary Of State Stimson for his work on the atomic project.

CAPT B·H·CHRISTENSON
SIGNAL CORPS

The Best Is Yet to Come

by General David Sarnoff

David Sarnoff in 1950 explored the science of electronics and predicted how it would help in the exploration of space.

We are just beginning to learn what electronics can do for man and mankind. We are just beginning to see the shape of the world to come. We glimpse new horizons as far as the mind can see.

The science of electronics deals with the behavior of electrons, those tiny electrical "particles" which travel across seemingly empty space with the speed of light. Radio and television are perhaps the best-known applications of electronics.

For many years we have been putting electronics to work to serve our creature needs. We have developed innumerable electronic devices. These may appear marvelous to us, and in a sense they are marvelous—but in reality they are only beginnings.

More recently we began to investigate the use of electronics to serve our bodies. In medicine, we have developed electronic methods of clinical diagnosis, quite similar to those used in a radio repair shop to diagnose the trouble with your radio. We observe and record heart action with an electrocardiograph, the functioning of the brain with an electroencephalograph, and pin-point cancerous cells by radioactive tracers. We are seeking to learn how to apply electronic radiations to repair and possibly rejuvenate living cells, safeguard health, and prolong life.

We have built electronic machines which can to some degree imitate the human brain: calculating, remembering, and even after a fashion thinking—faster and far more accurately than human brains can do.

The advance of science in all its branches—especially electronics—has been so vast and rapid that we humans sometimes find ourselves unprepared to live comfortably in a complex world of new machines.

We need a new education for the electronic age.

To educate, we must communicate knowledge, in a form that can be understood and remembered.

The important thing about electronics is that electrons can carry messages with the speed of light. Electronics is our means of instantaneous communication. The irony of our troubled world is that, with global means of instantaneous communication at our command, we discover we really communicate very little!

Individuals and nations do not understand each other. We live in a world of ideas, of complex concepts. Yet we try to communicate in words. We cannot use words alone to convey complex ideas with any precision.

Echoes from the moon are recorded by scientists at Bradley Beach, New Jersey.

Sarnoff was a pioneer in "sound on tape."

Not so long ago, within my own lifetime, there used to be a creature called "the well-read man." He is a rarity nowadays. For no man can read all the words printed today. But anyone's mind could absorb, comprehend, classify, and store for future reference all the new concepts and ideas represented by those words. The problem is to convey ideas with as few words as possible.

For example, you decide to walk across the room and turn on the radio. The gray matter of your brain receives this command and, without bothering your mind, instantly analyzes and details the complex logistics necessary for its execution. It flashes, in correct sequence, millions of impulses along the pathways of your nerves, causing your muscles to contract and relax, just so much and no more, each in its own turn. Through a different network of nerves, your brain receives reports from each muscle that the commands have been accurately obeyed. A third network of nerves transmits to the brain sensations of the changing picture of light, sound, feel, smell—"intelligence reports" which the brain notes and classifies, and when necessary changes its orders to the muscles. In a couple of seconds you have walked across the room and your fingers have flicked the switch. And this unbelievably complex operation, by an aggregate of cells far more numerous than the people of any nation, was accomplished by your deciding to walk across the room and turn on the radio. The minute details of how to fulfill that command were never the concern of your conscious mind. All that vast work was accurately performed by your subconscious or, if you prefer, your unconscious mind.

The capacity of the human mind, especially the subconscious mind, is far greater than we realize. We do not use more than a minute fraction of its capabilities. Our methods of education and training need to catch up with the march of science.

The old method of teaching—that is communicating ideas—began with the slow task of memorizing the individual letters of the alphabet, then painfully learning how to string letters into words, words into sentences, and then how to extract from them the small kernel of meaning which they contain. The modern method is to teach how to recognize entire words at a glance. This is a step in the right direction. We now also supplement words with pictures. That is an even more important step in the right direction.

Few Words Convey Ideas

In recent years the greatest advance in education was logged by our armed forces. To win the last war we had to train millions of individuals to use exceedingly complicated tools of warfare. The job had to be done in record time, yet the teaching had to be so thorough that the use of those tools became second nature, as easy as walking across the room and switching on the radio. The old-style textbooks would have been useless. So the armed services developed a new kind of textbook, the modern technical manual. This is a pictorial textbook: it communicates information through the use of step-by-step pictures, with the wordage reduced to a minimum. The pictures transmit to the mind new concepts—

David Sarnoff holds miniature TV camera to be used in man's exploration of space.

The inner works of one of first mechanical brains, used at Pennsylvania University.

not one at a time, but in short bursts of many related concepts simultaneously. This is a more direct method of communication, and the mind absorbs new data faster and remembers them more accurately.

A motion picture is an even more forceful way of communicating knowledge. The impact of moving pictures upon the human mind is tremendous. Modern civilization and the outlook on life have been greatly influenced by movies—at home and abroad.

Television, with its ability to transmit moving pictures of events instantaneously as they occur, and to reach millions simultaneously, will provide an even greater impact on the mind, especially the collective mind. Already, with only three million television receivers in operation, the impact of television upon our national life and individual habits is vital.

Speed of communications is a measure of the progress of civilization. Words alone are too slow to keep up with today's pace.

Ten years ago, in the Battle for Britain, the British radar warning net correlated reports from observers at many points in a matter of minutes. Today we do not have the minutes: we must deal in microseconds. With existing supersonic aircraft, and with the coming guided

Commander Howard Aiken, USNR, stands in front of his 1950 invention—world's largest computer.

missiles, we have no time for words—not even when those words are transmitted with the speed of light. Radar observations must be transmitted by coded pulses directly into electronic computers, which automatically flash resultant command pulses to interceptor aircraft a few microseconds later—without words and without human relays.

We found that it is useless to talk by radio to pilots of supersonic aircraft. By the time you finish talking, the airplane is nearly a hundred miles away. To meet these new needs a basically new system of communications had to be developed. Commands are transmitted in short bursts of pulses, not to the pilot, but to the airplane, and are automatically acknowledged by the airplane, not by the pilot. At the same instant the airplane's automatic transponder flashes the entire message to the pilot in a visual form, to be grasped at a glance and acted upon in a moment.

Researchers with differential analyzers at M.I.T.

Rocket To Moon

One of the great electronic discoveries in recent times was that radio waves travel beyond the earth. Four years ago the Signal Corps of the U. S. Army sent radar pulses to the moon, and some two and a half seconds later, after a round trip of nearly half a million miles, the echo blips registered on the radar-scope on earth. Electronics have bridged the gap between the earth and the moon.

One day we shall send an exploratory rocket to the moon. Satellite vehicles, giant rockets launched into space to patrol the earth as they whirl around it in their orbits like miniature moons, may become a reality. Electronics will guide these space ships in their courses and send back a wealth of new data. In a second or two, radio pulses will transmit voluminous observations, to be received here on earth in graphic form for visual study, pictures worth thousands of words.

Whether we want it or not, our lives are growing in complexity as time goes on. Yes we need new education for the electronic age. The key to that lies in the world-wide dissemination of ideas, and television may be a means to achieve that.

If I had my life to live over again, I think I should like to be born right now. We live in very interesting times. The best inventions are yet to be made, not only in electronics and nucleonics, but in the new humanities—geriatrics, the study of old age and prolongation of life; cybernetics, investigation of nerve and brain communication processes; radionetics, application of electronics in medicine, and other fields which are just beginning to unfold.

Immense opportunities are before us. The best is yet to be.

Portable TV sets were around as far back as 1948. This one had a 3½ inch screen.

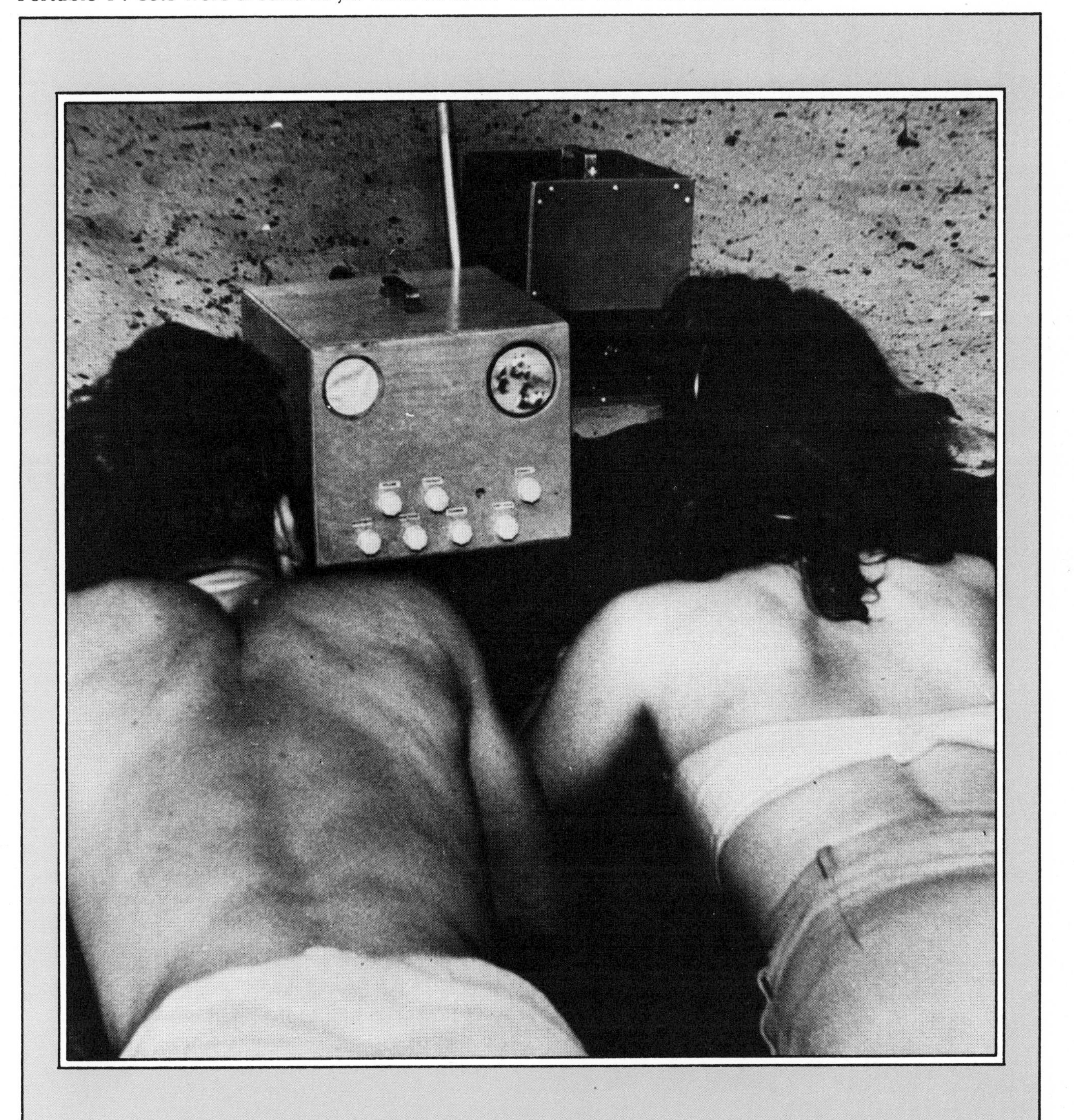

POLIOMYELITIS
DAVIS & CO.

Jonas Salk and the War Against Polio

The child and young adult crippled by polio was a common and sad sight in America before the mid-fifties. Jonas Salk, Albert Sabin, and their fellow researchers changed that to a rare sight, though still a sad one.

In many towns the church bells rang. Parents offered thankful prayers. In courts, judges interrupted trials for a moment of silent thanks.

Was it the end of a war? In a way it was, for Dr. Thomas Francis, eminent bacteriologist, had just announced that the Salk vaccine was safe, effective, and potent. Poliomyelitis (infantile paralysis) had been conquered by science. It was April 12, 1955, the tenth anniversary of the death of Franklin D. Roosevelt.

The date for the announcement had been deliberately chosen, for F.D.R. was the nation's most famous victim of the dread disease. In 1921, just a year after unsuccessfully running for Vice-President, he was stricken. He recovered, but was unable to get about normally for the rest of his life, 24 years.

Roosevelt, who was nearly 40 when stricken, was an exception to the general rule that by far the greatest number of polio victims are children, hence the popular name of infantile paralysis. The disease probably existed in ancient times, and Egyptian mummies bearing evidence of it have been found; but little was known about it until the last century.

By the twenties, people had heard and seen enough of the great crippler to live in fear for their children during the hot summer months. Some communities closed their swimming pools and movie houses during an epidemic, and parents everywhere kept their children away from crowds to safeguard them from polio.

The campaign against poliomyelitis began formally in 1937 with the announcement by Roosevelt that a new organization was being formed, the National Foundation for Infantile Paralysis. Roosevelt and a group of friends had been responsible for the purchase in 1926 of a property at Warm Springs, Georgia, and its transfer to a charitable foundation for the care of polio victims. To benefit the struggling foundation, the first annual President's Birthday Ball was held in 1934.

Manager of the original foundation, then head of the new organization was Basil O'Connor, law partner of Franklin Roosevelt. When the National Foundation was formed in 1937, scientists had been searching for some years for a vaccine that would defeat the crippler. Two such vaccines, crude in form, had already been developed by Dr. Maurice Brodie of New York University and by Dr. John Kolmer of Temple University. Virus studies by Dr. Albert B. Sabin at Rockefeller Institute in New York were to lead him into the search for a polio vaccine a few years later.

Dr. Salk (r) discovered anti-polio serum.

After its discovery in 1954, Salk's anti-polio vaccine was rushed to all parts of country.

On that memorable April morning in 1955, Dr. Jonas Salk was not quite 41 years old. He had been born in New York City, the son of an Orthodox Jew who worked in the garment district. The family was poor, but determined that the sons should go to college and then enter professions.

Jonas was a brilliant student and was graduated from high school at the age of 15. He entered City College to take a pre-law course, but soon discovered a burning interest in science. After graduating from C.C.N.Y. at the age of 19, he enrolled at N.Y.U.'s College of Medicine, planning to go on to medical research. Here he learned about the polio vaccines of Brodie and Kolmer. He learned, too, about the controversy over live and killed virus in the vaccine.

Work At Michigan, Pitt

In 1939 Salk was graduated from medical school, but remained there for a time on a fellowship, working under Dr. Thomas Francis. During his senior year he had also worked under Dr. Francis, and they had discovered that it was possible to kill a virus without destroying its ability to produce antibodies. Their belief was that such a killed virus injected into a body could cause a buildup of antibodies and protect the patient from the disease. This theory was to have a tremendous influence on Salk's work when in 1942 he received a fellowship grant from the five-year-old National Foundation.

That same year Dr. Francis had moved to the University of Michigan, and Salk joined him there. He stayed for five years before growing tired of being an assistant professor. What he really wanted was his own laboratory. He was becoming known in his field and sensed that this was the time to look around.

For a while he had no success, but at last was offered a position at the University of Pittsburgh School of Medicine, which was then recruiting full-time faculty members for research. The situation at Pitt proved disappointing at first, but Dr. Salk eventually found his opportunity.

It had been known since the early thirties that there was probably more than one strain of polio, but nobody knew how many. A polio vaccine would be almost useless unless it conferred immunity on all strains, so the National Foundation set out on the tedious process of classifying all strains. Salk joined a group of prominent scientists on this project. By 1951 the researchers had established that there were three strains. Now Salk could go ahead with his search for a vaccine.

Acting on his belief and that of Dr. Francis, Dr. Salk set out to insure safety of the proposed vaccine by killing the virus. He had to find a way to do this without destroying its ability to produce antibodies. He achieved this by "cooking" the liquid virus culture at a ratio of 4,000 to 1 of formaldehyde at body temperature. To be absolutely sure, he continued the process for nine days. At the end of that time, he was convinced, it was safe.

Tests With Humans

Up to this time, monkeys had been used in the study. Now it was necessary to find out whether the injection of killed viruses would increase antibodies in humans. Salk was granted permission to experiment with some children who had previously had polio. He was heartened by the fact that there were no adverse effects whatever while the antibody count shot up dramatically. He then extended experiments to those who had never had polio, and again was successful.

While Dr. Salk was preparing a paper on his findings to be published in the Journal of the American Medical Association, word of the apparently successful vaccine leaked out to a newspaper columnist, who printed it. O'Connor and Salk decided the only thing to do was to put the whole story before the public. This they did in a televised speech by Salk in March 1953. In it he outlined the history of polio and the fight against it. He assured parents that there would be a vaccine, but that the work had to proceed cautiously.

Parents across the nation hailed the announcement. Now they had hope. Physicians and other scientists were more restrained. The doctors were angry because the public was told before Salk's findings were reported to them officially. The other scientists accused him of seeking publicity.

Meanwhile Salk continued his experiments. Two months after the television appearance he vaccinated himself and his own family, then a group of children in two well-to-do Pittsburgh suburbs. Now Salk started pressing O'Connor for a mass test. Finally O'Connor announced that before the 1954 polio season a half million to a million second-grade children would be

During polio epidemic in Chicago children were given free injections of Salk vaccine.

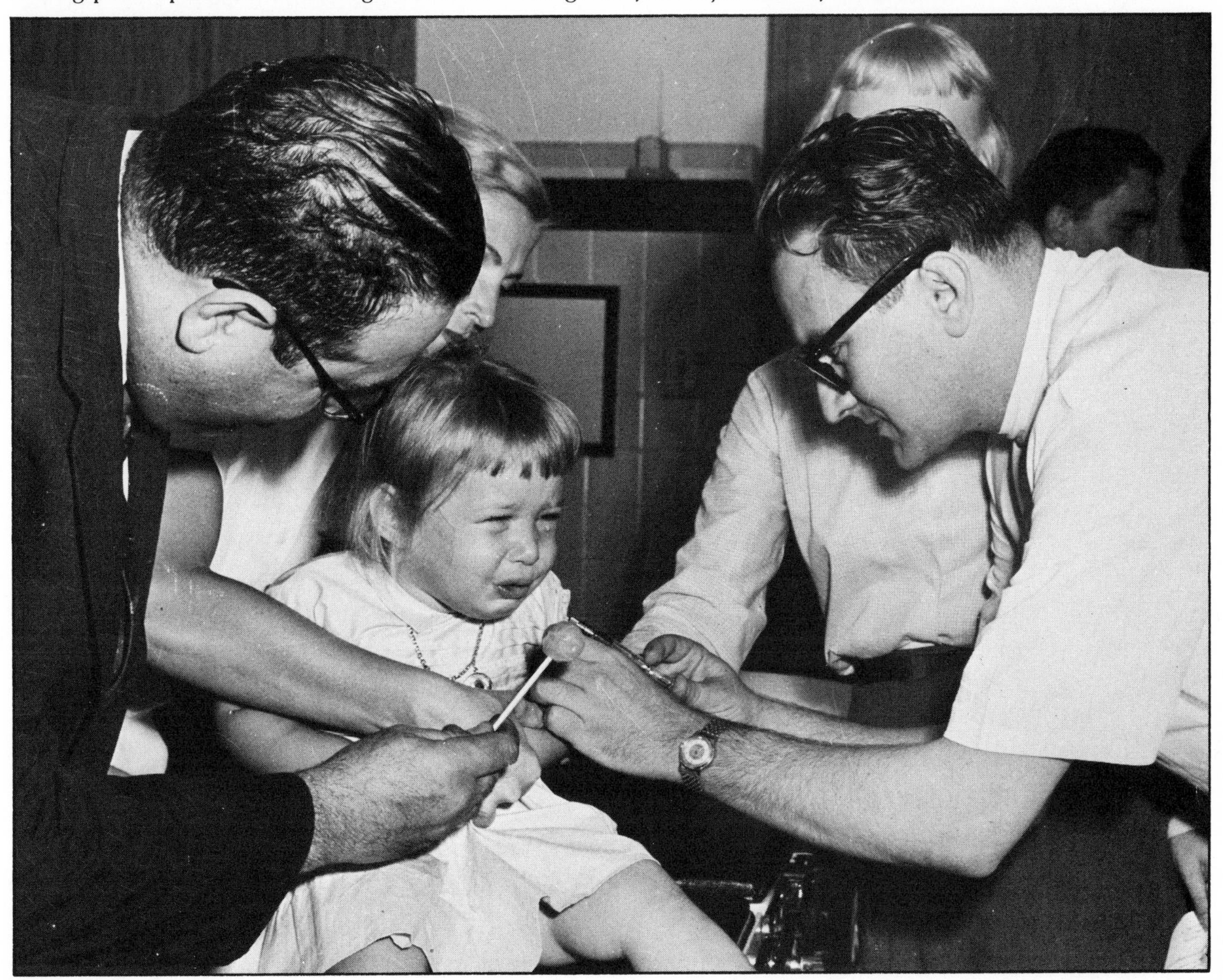

(Above) Dr. Salk explains production of vaccine. (Below) Dr. Salk with family on eve of announcement that his vaccine was 80 to 90% effective against polio.

tested, in every case with written permission from the parents.

The war seemed to be near its end, but there were still battles to be fought. One battle—over the killing of polio virus with formaldehyde—was brought about by one doctor's report that he had been unsuccessful with the method. Other doctors stated that there had not been a thorough enough study of the Salk vaccine, that it was being pushed ahead too rapidly.

Further Skirmishing

The method of testing came under attack, too. Instead of contrasting the number of cases of polio within the vaccinated group with non-vaccinated children in the same community, many doctors wanted the placebo method. For this, dummy doses would be given to some children while others would be given the real vaccine. The latter method was chosen, and Dr. Francis named to administer it.

The test began in April 1954, and one year

Marion Folsom, Secretary of HEW presents Dr. Salk with medal.

later Dr. Francis made the dramatic announcement that the vaccine developed by Dr. Salk was 80-90 percent effective against paralytic poliomyelitis.

Now the war really did seem to be over, but there were still scientific skirmishes and setbacks. That same year a batch of defective serum produced by a California pharmaceutical firm caused the death or crippling of a number of children. But there was a steady decrease of polio cases in the United States down to 40 in 1967.

Then came another skirmish, equally serious. It was a revival of the killed-versus-live virus controversy. This time it involved Dr. Albert B. Sabin, a critic of Dr. Salk, and an advocate of live vaccine.

Dr. Sabin, eight years older than Dr. Salk, is a Russian Jew. He studied dentistry at N.Y.U., then switched to medicine and was graduated as an M.D. in 1931. He said that Salk's vaccine would require multiple doses and yearly boosters. His, he claimed, would confer lifetime immunity after three doses. It also had the advantage of being administered orally on lumps of sugar instead of requiring a needle.

The National Foundation supported Sabin's research also, but was more cautious than it had been in the case of Salk. Tests on prisoners at a federal reformatory were successful, but the U.S. Public Health Service did not license it until 1962.

Meanwhile Russia had adopted the Sabin vaccine. In 1962, Great Britain as well as the United States accepted it. Now both are used in the West while Russia uses the Sabin vaccine exclusively.

In the United States today, the Sabin vaccine, because it is easy to administer, is used more widely. But parents who had small children in 1955 still look back thankfully to that memorable day when they learned that Jonas Salk and his colleagues had conquered the great crippler; and younger parents can relax with the knowledge that one more disease is under control.

Wernher Von Braun, Space Age Giant

He came to prominence as the leading figure in the development of the Nazi rocket launching center at Peenemünde, Germany. Today an American citizen, Wernher von Braun is one of the architects of the U.S. space program.

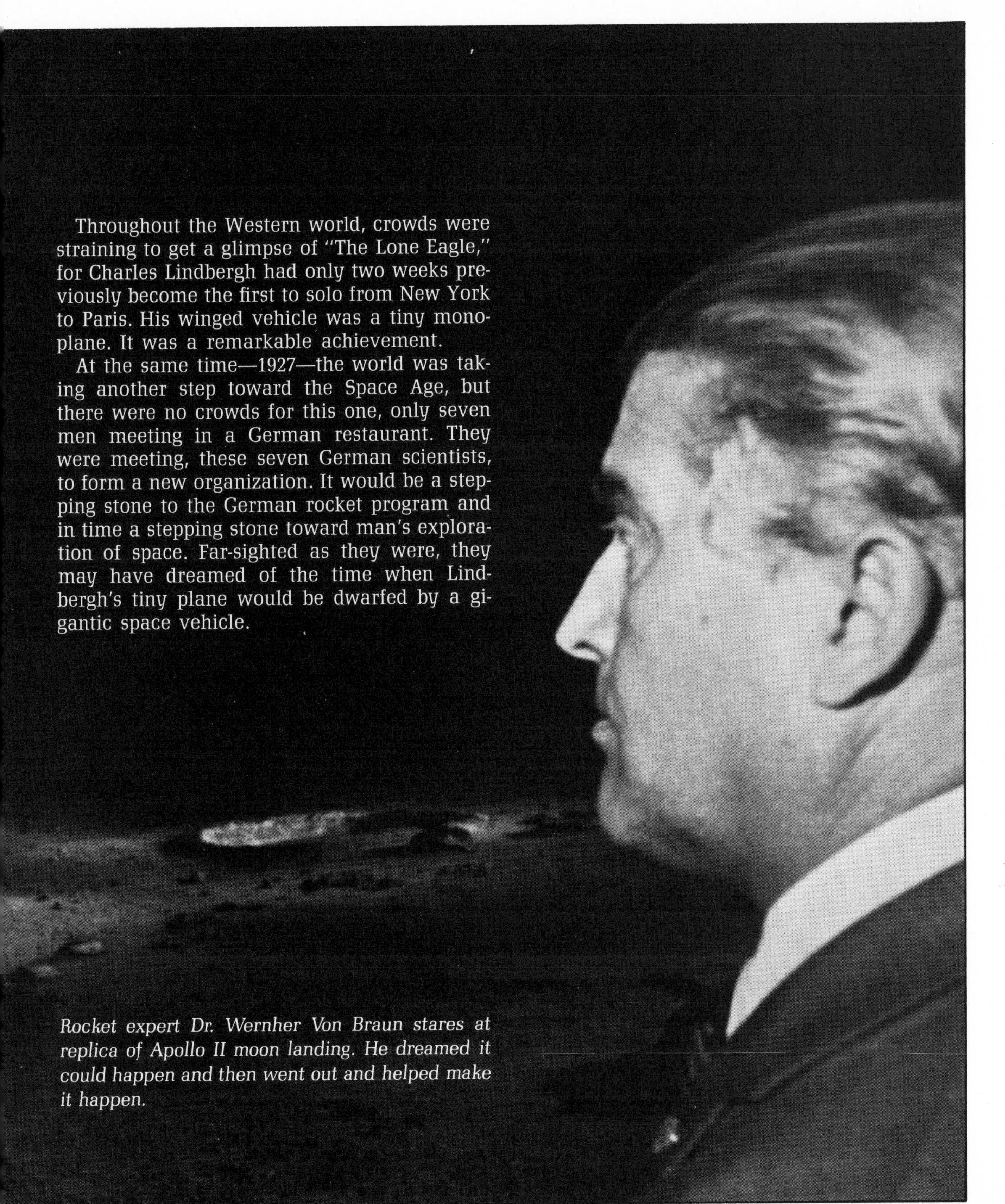

Throughout the Western world, crowds were straining to get a glimpse of "The Lone Eagle," for Charles Lindbergh had only two weeks previously become the first to solo from New York to Paris. His winged vehicle was a tiny monoplane. It was a remarkable achievement.

At the same time—1927—the world was taking another step toward the Space Age, but there were no crowds for this one, only seven men meeting in a German restaurant. They were meeting, these seven German scientists, to form a new organization. It would be a stepping stone to the German rocket program and in time a stepping stone toward man's exploration of space. Far-sighted as they were, they may have dreamed of the time when Lindbergh's tiny plane would be dwarfed by a gigantic space vehicle.

Rocket expert Dr. Wernher Von Braun stares at replica of Apollo II moon landing. He dreamed it could happen and then went out and helped make it happen.

Dr. Von Braun and other German scientists surrendered to U.S. troops in World War II.

The seven named themselves Verein für Raumschiffahrt (Society for Space Travel, later referred to as the German Rocket Society). They already had their eyes on the stars, and two years after its founding the society had attracted nearly 1,000 other members whose heads were also above the clouds. One of these was Wernher von Braun, the seventeen-year-old son of the Baron and Baroness Magnus Freiherr von Braun.

The Baron had at one time been Minister of Agriculture. His wife was an enthusiastic amateur astronomer, who presented her son with an unusual gift when he was confirmed in the Lutheran church—a telescope. Young Wernher was excited by the telescope and the new views of the heavens it brought him. It was not long before he decided he wanted to explore space, not just look at it through a telescope.

The VfR, as it came to be called, needed a base for its experiments. Its members were overjoyed when they were able to rent for almost nothing an abandoned ammunition dump on the outskirts of Berlin and they set out to repair two of its bunkers and to clear the tangle of weeds from its 300 acres. They named it Raketenflugplatz Berlin (Rocket Field Berlin).

The project was coming along nicely by 1931, when Hitler began his rise. The rocket enthusiasts were far more interested in space than they were in politics, so they did not regard the visit of three officers from German Army Ordinance in 1932 as an omen of things to come. The officers made young von Braun an offer he could hardly refuse, the chance to study for a degree at the University of Berlin under a professor who was also in the Ordinance Department. The offer carried with it the opportunity to use Army facilities for the necessary experimental work. Wernher von Braun accepted the offer and worked for his degree and then his doctorate in physics as a civilian employee of the Army.

German militarists of the early thirties had already realized that the Treaty of Versailles in its disarmament provisions had left them a loophole, for who could have seriously considered rockets as weapons of war at the time the treaty was drafted? Hence their interest in the VfR and its experimenters. The idea they had was to develop a rocket comparable to the huge gun used against Paris in World War I, the Paris Gun, called Big Bertha by some.

Peenemunde

A site for the production and firing of such a weapon was needed, and the young civilian employee von Braun was asked to look around. It had to be an isolated area, relatively safe from attack, and almost uninhabited. Von Braun eventually remembered that his father had at one time gone duck-hunting on the island of Usedom on the Baltic Sea. It seemed a promising site for a rocket base, and eventually the Nazis set up their rocket base at Peenemünde ("Mouth of the Peene") on Usedom.

This was to be the launching site for the dreaded V-2 Rocket, a leading developer of which was von Braun. While it was being readied for a heavy attack on England, London was being subjected to a "robot blitz" of smaller rockets, V-1's. In September 1944 the V-2's started falling on England and continued for seven months. During that time over 1,300 V-2s fell on English soil, killing nearly 3,000 people and seriously injuring nearly twice that number. The newspapers took to calling it "Hitler's Rocket," but it appears that he was not nearly so much interested in the rocket program as in other phases of his war. The R.A.F. made Peenemünde a primary target, but did not succeed in knocking it out completely, though it is probable that their bombings cut down the number of V-2's fired.

Dr. Wernher von Braun was the civilian engineer in charge of the rocket program at Peenemünde, while the commanding officer of the installation was General Walter Dornberger. In March of 1944, Dornberger found it necessary to intercede with Nazi authorities to save the lives of von Braun and two engineers, who were arrested and charged with sabotage. They had been overheard saying that they had to work on the rocket but their real objective was space travel. To the Nazis this constituted sabotage of the rocket program for they reasoned that the whole energy of the trio was not being applied to the rocket. A more serious charge was that von Braun was plotting to escape to England in the small plane he used for inspection flights.

The real story behind the arrests hinged on Heinrich Himmler's desire to get as many of the war projects as he could under the jurisdic-

General J. B. Medaris (l) and Dr. Von Braun were instrumental in launching the first satellite.

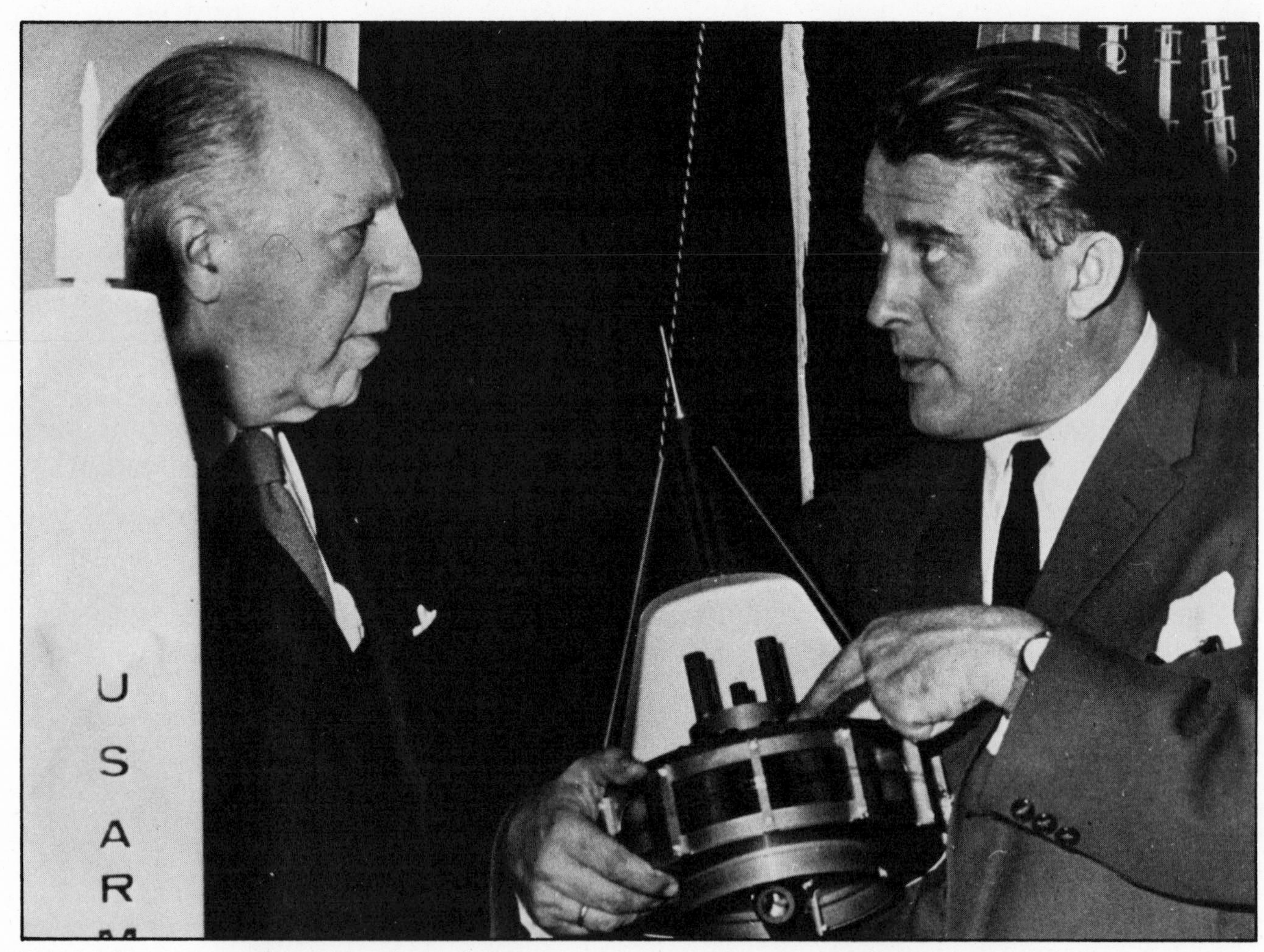

Dr. Von Braun (r) explains launching of Pioneer IV to Army Secretary Wilber Brucker.

tion of his SS. The previous year, he had visited Peenemünde and had taken von Braun aside, suggesting that it would be better if the V-2 project were taken away from the Army and given to the SS. Von Braun refused to go along with the scheme, and it nearly cost him his life. The three rocket scientists were released only after General Dornberger declared under oath that they were needed for the completion of the V-2 project.

While sabotage seems too strong a word, there seems to be little doubt that the rocket developers were more interested in space than in earthly weapons of war. Von Braun is reported to have commented after the first V-2 landed in England that it landed on the wrong planet.

As the Western Allies and the Russians closed in on Germany from both sides in 1945, the rocket scientists faced a new threat. The planning committee was sent to Bavaria, where they were housed at a plush ski resort. Though they were comfortable physically, their state of mind was not improved by the rumors that the secret police had orders to liquidate them rather than allow them to fall into Allied hands.

Race For Space

They knew that the war had ended for Germany and understood that the ski resort was surrounded by American troops, so they sent Magnus, Wernher's brother, to try to find a patrol to whom they could surrender. Magnus, who spoke English well, bicycled down the hill until he met an American soldier, whom he persuaded to take him to the nearby headquarters of the Counter Intelligence Corps. In the confusion, the officer in charge had not been notified that top priority was to be given to locating and taking into custody the developers of the V-2, so he just told Magnus to bring them all back the next morning.

By the next day, the Allies realized what a treasure trove of scientific brains had fallen into their hands. Asked later why he had chosen the American side, von Braun replied that he and his team members believed that the American system would safeguard individual rights and that the knowledge the scientists entrusted to the Americans would not be misused.

Now the Allies and von Braun had to choose the hundred or more team members who would go to the United States. Meanwhile the rocket factory had been captured, and the Americans, moving fast, loaded three box cars with rocket components and put them on ships headed across the Atlantic.

En route to the United States, von Braun had a stopover in England, where he was much impressed by the courtesy accorded him by Sir Alwyn Crowe, developer of the British rockets. Only four years later, von Braun was invited to become an Honorary Fellow of the British Interplanetary Society, which seemed to bear out his observation that Westerners did not hold the grudges he would expect in his own country.

The destination of the rocket scientists was White Sands Proving Grounds in New Mexico. They were to be based at El Paso, Texas. Getting von Braun, an enemy alien in military custody, across the country by train so soon after V-E Day was a tricky operation, but it was accomplished without incident.

The rocket team was soon settled at Fort Bliss and working on rockets for their new homeland. It was to be a new homeland for them, for they applied for American citizenship as soon as legally possible. In 1947 their wives and children were brought to the United States, and von Braun was granted permission to return to Bavaria to marry. His bride was an eighteen-year-old second cousin.

The years following the war were busy ones for von Braun and his team, first at White Sands, then later at Huntsville, Alabama, where he became director of the program at Redstone Arsenal that produced the Jupiter rocket. In 1970 he joined the staff of the National Aeronautics and Space Administration (NASA).

Escape To U.S.

The events of the 1950's jarred Americans and made them aware of the need for constant vigilance. The first was the Korean War, which caused a jump in allocations for armaments, including rockets. At that time von Braun was moved to Huntsville, where there was a spurt of frenzied activity at the Redstone Arsenal. Then in 1957 the Russians launched Sputnik, and the world entered the Space Age.

When the Russians successfully orbited Sputnik I, there was a storm of criticism within the United States, for our space technicians had been struggling to overcome the bugs in the Vanguard program, and we were yet to have a successful launch. Then three months after the first shot by the Russians, the United States got its Explorer I into orbit.

Now the United States was in the race. In 1959 Wernher von Braun reported to a Congressional committee that he thought man would fly around the moon in the following decade. He estimated that man would land on the moon itself a few years thereafter. The estimate, it turned out, was on the cautious side.

In 1959, a space vehicle from the Soviet Union looped behind the moon to take pictures. Two years later, Russia's Yuri Gagarin orbited the earth; and the same year the U.S. put the first of its Mercury astronauts into suborbital flight, using the powerful rockets developed at the Redstone Arsenal. The next year John Glenn became the first American in orbit.

In 1964 a United States space shot hit the moon, its cameras sending out over 4,000 pictures in the last few minutes before impact. In 1966, both the United States and the U.S.S.R. sent aloft vehicles that made soft landings and sent back pictures. They both also put vehicles in orbit around the moon.

Then, in 1969, a decade after von Braun's report to the Congressional committee, man first stood on the moon. Rocketry had come a long way since man first dreamed of exploring space; and Wernher von Braun had come a long way since he first looked through that gift telescope.